Lynda Field is a trained therapist who specializes in personal and group development. She is the author of nine titles, including the bestselling *60 Ways to Feel Amazing* and *60 Ways to Change Your Life*. In addition to giving seminars and workshops, she writes a column for a major Internet provider, as well as articles for a variety of national magazines. She lives in Essex, UK.

Visit Lynda online at www.lyndafield.com

By the same author:

60 Ways to Change Your Life

60 Ways to Feel Amazing

The Little Book of Woman Power

60 Tips for Self-Esteem

Creating Self-Esteem

60 Ways to Heal Your Life

More than 60 Ways to Make Your Life Amazing

The Self-Esteem Workbook

Self-Esteem for Women

A Practical Guide to Love, Intimacy and Success

Lynda Field

Vermilion
LONDON

5 7 9 10 8 6 4

First published in 1997 by Element Books.
This edition published in 2001 by Vermilion,
an imprint of Ebury Press, Random House,
20 Vauxhall Bridge Road, London SW1V 2SA
www.randomhouse.co.uk

Random House Australia (Pty) Limited
20 Alfred Street, Milsons Point, Sydney,
New South Wales 2061, Australia

Random House New Zealand Limited
18 Poland Road, Glenfield,
Auckland 10, New Zealand

Random House South Africa (Pty) Limited
Endulini, 5A Jubilee Road,
Parktown 2193, South Africa

The Random House Group Limited Reg. No. 954009

Papers used by Vermilion are natural, recyclable
products made from wood grown in sustainable forests.

Printed and bound in Great Britain by Bookmarque Ltd,
Croydon, Surrey

A CIP catalogue record for this book
is available from the British Library

ISBN 0-09-187632-X

Contents

DEDICATED TO MY DAUGHTER,
LEILA PORTER

Acknowledgements

To my wonderful husband Richard for his care, support, integrity and love – thank you for everything.

To my daughter Leilah and my sons Jack and Alex whose high spirits help me to keep my sense of humour when the pressure is on – thanks for being such great children.

Thank you to my parents Barbara and Idwal Goronwy who taught me to be creative.

Thank you to Mary Field, my mother-in-law, for her delightful company, her beautiful garden and her delicious puddings.

And my grateful appreciation to all the wonderful women in my life who have shared their ups and downs with me.

Preface

A woman with self-esteem takes herself seriously. She recognizes her own worth and knows that she deserves the very best that life can offer her; she is aware of her own desires and works towards fulfilling her needs; she respects her feelings and is prepared to express them; and she is ready to take responsibility for creating relationships which encourage and support her high self-esteem.

Are you a woman with self-esteem? If your answer is 'no', you are one of the vast majority and this book is for you. Why do we find it so hard to believe in ourselves? Why are we so self-critical? How can we change the way we feel about ourselves? Over the past few years I have run many courses on developing self-esteem. The workshops have been open to both women and men, but usually the ratio of attendance is one man to ten women. At every single workshop there has developed a lively and sometimes fiery discussion about the different issues facing men and women in the quest for self-esteem.

These are some of the things that women have said:

- It's harder for women to believe in themselves.
- Looking after children isn't seen as a worthwhile job.
- Society takes men more seriously than women.
- I have to fight every day to prove myself equal to my male peers at work.
- I supported my husband and children for 20 years – they have careers and a place in society and I feel I've got nothing.
- However hard I try, I find myself feeling intimidated by men.

- I always end up being angry with the men in my life, they seem to have it so easy.

These are some of the things that men have said:

- Women find it easier to look at the issue of self-esteem.
- Men are expected to take care of women; it seems wrong to start trying to care for myself.
- It is difficult for me to look at my own feelings and impossible for me to discuss them with other men.
- I can only talk about my feelings of self-worth with women; other men just don't want to know.
- I'm a bit lost in this 'new man' image; I try to support my partner, but I feel guilty every time I do something for myself – I feel guilty about being a man.

The ways that we think, feel and behave create the quality of our lives. If you think that you are 'not good enough', you will feel inadequate, incapable and lacking in confidence and your behaviour will reflect these feelings; you will be one of life's victims and you will be very low in self-esteem. If you have self-belief and can love and value yourself, in spite of your mistakes, you will feel empowered to go out into the world to get what you want; you will be high in self-esteem.

The precise ways in which we think, feel and act can be described as our 'patterns'. We learn many patterns in our very early childhood – we learn 'ways of coping with things'. Many of us repeat these patterns (ways of coping) in our adult life. The vital question to ask here is whether your patterns of thinking, feeling and behaving create high or low self-esteem.

We learn what to believe about ourselves when we are very tiny. We listen to the people around us – first our families and then other figures outside our home. We are taught by our families and by our society to believe certain things about ourselves and about our world. For many centuries our society has been patriarchal. This has created problems for both sexes as we have learned to fulfil our culturally defined roles. Traditionally expected male patterns of behaviour have seriously affected the ways in which many men relate, both to their own emotions and to the feelings of others. At the same time, the expectations of a male-led society have made it difficult for many women to be able to act powerfully and assertively.

Yes, women and men are different! Eventually every workshop debate concludes that our individual levels of self-esteem are influenced by our close families and also by our cultural rules. In other words, everyone has their own personal journey towards self-esteem, but the nature of the route will be determined by whether we are female or male.

I like to know not just *why* something is, but also *how* it got to be like that; what is the process behind it and *how it can be changed*. Each woman is unique with her own set of patterns, and yet we share a cultural and biological bond which creates a recognizable thread running through the female quest for self-esteem.

Why does my womanhood often stand in the way of my self-belief? How did this happen to me? How can I change this situation into one where being a woman empowers my life and supports my self-esteem? Discover the answers to these questions and become a truly creative, fulfilled and empowered woman. Become a woman with self-esteem.

A New Way of Looking at Our Womanhood

You are a strong and powerful woman. You are thoughtful, intuitive, resourceful, sensitive and creative, and when you bring all of these qualities together you feel confident, alive, energetic, successful, assertive and empowered.

Perhaps you don't feel like a strong and powerful woman. In the space below, write down what you see when you look at yourself.

....

....

Would you like to change the way you see yourself?

You are made up of more than just your physical body. You have highly developed spiritual, emotional and mental qualities and you experience every moment of your life with your mind, body, spirit and emotions.

Look at yourself in the mirror and become aware of the different levels of your experience:

- **Mind** – Observe your thoughts.
- **Body** – See your physical presence.
- **Spirit** – Be aware of your spiritual connection.
- **Emotions** – Acknowledge your feelings.

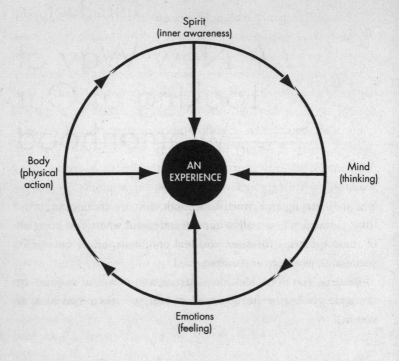

Figure 1 A total experience

What thoughts and feelings did you experience? Did they support your self-esteem or not?

Every event in our lives is responded to by our mind, body, spirit and emotions. These levels of awareness affect each other and act together to create our experiences (see Figure 1). Think of a time when you were high in self-esteem; your energy was flowing freely, your mind was thinking positively, you were in touch with your own feelings, you acted assertively and you were aware of your spirituality. We feel good when we are high in self-esteem because our energies are balanced and in harmony.

High self-esteem can change very quickly into low self-esteem. We can all relate to this. One minute you are balanced, centred, in control and feeling good, then suddenly you've lost it – down you go, feeling worthless, useless and uncomfortable. Your self-esteem has gone because your energies are out of balance. Your energy is blocked somewhere and this will affect the quality of your total experience. Certain types of patterns (of thought, feelings and behaviour) block energy and so create low self-esteem. We will have learned such patterns when we were young and they will affect our levels of self-esteem as adults.

Whenever you feel worthless, think that you are no good or act like a victim, you are allowing a negative pattern to run your life. A negative pattern is one which creates low self-esteem by blocking your energy so that you are not feeling centred and balanced. Throughout this book we will be looking closely at the patterns which can inhibit our freedom of mental, physical, emotional and spiritual expression. We can change all the patterns which don't work for us into new positive patterns which support and empower us. First we need to become aware of ourselves. Self-awareness is the key to self-change and is the mother of self-esteem: self-awareness *creates* self-esteem.

The quality of our total experience depends upon the balanced interrelationship between mind, body, spirit and emotions. Any negative thought, emotional or behavioural pattern will produce an experience of low self-esteem. Building self-esteem is a very personal issue which involves surmounting our individual obstacles to belief in ourselves. Our individual challenges are very closely linked to our sex. Here we could very easily become involved in (and distracted by) a debate about the meaning of a woman's role within a male-dominated society. There is indeed much to talk about and this book will address many women's issues within this context. However, at this point I would like to suggest a new way of looking at your womanhood – a way which will empower you to create high self-esteem in all areas of your life, not *in spite* of being a woman but *because* of being a woman.

Ancient eastern philosophies and modern western psychology have taught that we each have male and female energies within us. Both men and women are a combination of female and male energy. The feminine energies within us represent our receptivity, the intuitive part of our nature. Our masculine energies represent our active principle. When mind, body, spirit and emotions are working in harmony, then our male and female energies are balanced. Our female energy receives information at the spiritual and emotional level. Female energy is wise and instinctive and we become aware of it through our intuition. We then use our male energy to take this creative impulse and express it in appropriate action. Remember that we are talking about inner processes here. Both men and women who are high in self-esteem will be using a balance of their female and male energies in the creative process.

FEMALE ENERGY + MALE ENERGY → CREATIVE PROCESS

Think of a time when you felt a strong impulse to do something, then you acted on that impulse and were pleased with the result – it had a sense of rightness to it. This is an example of your male and female energies working in harmony. Figure 2 shows how our female energies lie along the axis of spirituality and emotions, while our male energies connect our mind (thought processes) with physical action. High self-esteem involves balancing mind, body, spirit and emotions, and for this to happen our own male and female energies must be in harmony.

Society does not encourage us to recognize our inner male and female energies; we are taught to believe that our thought and action processes (male energy) are all-important and we learn to control, suppress and even deny our female energy (spiritual and emotional awareness). The inner male dominates the inner female. Both women and men elevate the status of their inner male and deny the power of their inner female. This gross inner imbalance is reflected within our culture. Our traditionally male-dominated society has suppressed and controlled women, with the result that women have lost self-respect and self-esteem. Powerful negative cultural patterns have ensured that as women we have lost the sense of the vital, intuitive and wise female energy which we need to guide our actions to a successful conclusion.

Self-awareness creates self-esteem, and becoming aware means that we need to look closely at the ways in which we have been influenced, both by our family and by our society. We learn ways of believing, thinking, feeling and behaving by absorbing messages in our very early childhood. We can think of these messages as

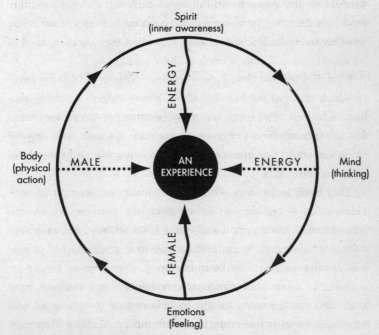

Figure 2 Male and female energy

our *family patterns* which will be unique for each of us.

Our traditional society supports many myths and fantasies about womanhood. As women, we share the influence of a culture which for so many centuries has treated us as second-class citizens. This legacy of beliefs has created strong and obvious messages about what it means to be a woman in our society. We have internalized many of these expectations (including the *lack* of expectations) and have made them our very own. We can think of these messages as our *cultural patterns*.

The nature of our beliefs, thoughts, feelings and emotions are influenced by a mixture of our unique family patterns and our cultural patterns. Family and cultural influences are interdependent, but in this book we will often separate them in order to gain greater insight into specific areas of low self-esteem. These two threads, family patterns and cultural patterns, run through this book together. Negative family and cultural patterns often come together to create low self-esteem and when they do they need to be unravelled and traced back to their source.

Why do I believe that I am worthless? Where did I learn this? In which areas of my life do I allow others to treat me as worthless? Who and what supports my self esteem? How can I increase my self-esteem in every area of my life? We can only answer these questions for ourselves when we untangle the threads of our own patterning.

This book is for any woman who wants to be high in self-esteem. It will enable you to recognize the patterns which you have learned from your family and from society. Become self-aware, and change your critical negative patterns for others which offer support and self-esteem. Embrace your power by learning to trust yourself. Learn to develop and balance your male and female energies so that your mind, body, spirit and emotions work in harmony with each other. Reclaim your self-respect and self-esteem and create the life you deserve.

Part 1
Patterning

1

Women as Daughters – Family Patterns

There's naught good nor bad,
but thinking makes it so.

(WILLIAM SHAKESPEARE, HAMLET)

This tale began a long time ago, when you were born. In your mind's eye, see yourself as a tiny baby lying in your cradle. It may be very hard to imagine your babyhood in this way, but you really were once your mother and father's beautiful baby daughter. Look into this cradle. What do you see? How would you describe yourself? Beautiful, pure, perfect, innocent, tender, vulnerable, full of wonder and love, trusting and open-hearted. Your birth was a miracle. Now come back to the present moment and describe yourself. Just write down the first words which come to mind.

I am:

....

....

Where has the trust and perfection gone? What has happened to you? Nothing has changed; you have just grown up. You are still your parents' beautiful daughter. You may be experiencing a lot of conflicting emotions as you think about yourself in this way.

Many thoughts and feelings are stirred when we start to think in positive and self-loving ways about ourselves. As babies we unquestionably recognized our right to be here; we were fascinated by everything we experienced; we found ourselves infinitely fascinating. If you find this hard to believe about yourself, just look at a baby. Look into that baby's eyes; what do you see there?

You were born with a sense of purpose; you were prepared to enjoy the adventure of your life; you believed in yourself and you were high in self-esteem. What has happened to you since?

There is really no great mystery surrounding your life. You may feel caught up in many complicated issues, and things might seem impossible to resolve – but they aren't! Life is really very simple: we create for ourselves what we think we deserve, and whatever we believe to be true about ourselves becomes true for us.

This truth has profound implications. As you work through this book, you will begin to recognize certain patterns of thoughts, feelings and behaviour which keep recurring in your life. If these patterns have a negative influence on the quality of your life, then they can be changed.

If your mind is full of self-loathing, then remember that you are only dealing with a thought that you are a despicable person. You have believed this thought and have created all sorts of emotions which support your self-hatred. The feelings are real, and match the thought. Figure 3 demonstrates how a negative thought pattern creates corresponding feelings and behaviour which together ensure low self-esteem. You believe yourself to be a truly terrible person, you feel absolutely awful about yourself, you don't deserve to be treated well – and so you won't be. Thoughts of self-hatred produce an amazing array of oppressive feelings, such as guilt, shame, resentment, anger and fear. Such feelings ensure that we create for ourselves a complicated and

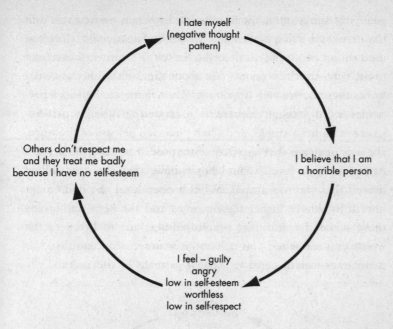

Figure 3 How a negative thought pattern creates low self-esteem

confusing life full of punishment and blame. If you subscribe to such negative feelings, then you will feel worthless. The people in your life will pick up on this feeling and will treat you as worthless. If you think that you are no good, it won't be long before everyone agrees with you. It isn't difficult to 'prove' your 'inadequacies'.

If you are low in self-esteem, your mind is full of negative thoughts about yourself. You are not a bad, worthless, useless, undeserving person. Why do you ever believe these things to be true about yourself? They are not true; you only believe them to be true – truth and belief are not necessarily the same!

Claire is a lawyer with two children. She is bright and energetic, but she is often low in self-esteem. When we first met and Claire told me about herself and her family background, she often used the word 'stupid' to describe herself. I listen very carefully to the ways in which people talk about themselves, as the actual words they use are very important. When someone repeats a particular word form, it represents a repeating thought pattern. Claire is far from stupid, and when I queried her use of the word, she was unaware that she frequently used it to describe herself. At a conscious level, Claire didn't know that she kept telling herself that she was stupid, but at a deep level she had taught herself to believe in her inadequacies and she kept reinforcing these beliefs by affirming her stupidity. Start to listen to the words you use when you talk about yourself; you can discover many unconscious negative thought patterns by this method.

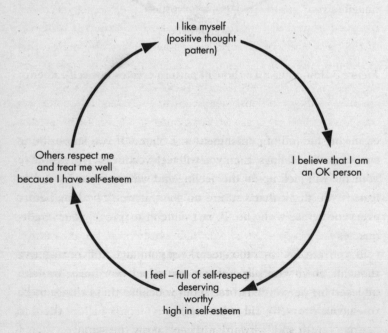

I like myself
(positive thought
pattern)

I believe that I am
an OK person

I feel – full of self-respect
deserving
worthy
high in self-esteem

Others respect me
and treat me well
because I have self-esteem

Figure 4 How a positive thought pattern creates high self-esteem

If you change a negative thought pattern into a positive one, the whole process is affected. Figure 4 shows how a positive thought can create high self-esteem. If you like yourself and believe that you are OK, you will feel deserving, worthy and full of self-esteem and people will treat you with the respect that you feel you deserve. This sounds so simple and yet is such a profound truth. The key to self-change lies in self-awareness. When we become conscious of the negative patterns by which we run our lives it becomes possible to change these patterns so that our beliefs, thoughts and feelings about ourselves become positively supportive.

FAMILY MESSAGES

Imagine your mind as a book in which everything has been recorded from the moment you were born. By the age of three, this book was full of all sorts of messages. (We will develop this idea more fully in the chapter explaining affirmations.) Our strongest beliefs are based on the things we hear very early on in our lives and so our most significant messages usually come via our parents and siblings. At workshops we 'brainstorm' to discover our own childhood messages. Everyone calls out anything that they can remember from their early years which might have influenced the quality of their lives. We cover pages and pages of paper with such messages: be nice; be perfect; stop crying; don't behave like a boy; you are so fat; so ugly; lazy; unkind; thoughtless; a waste of space; I wish you hadn't been born; I never wanted you; you are too noisy; too quiet; keep your anger to yourself; act normally; know your place; if only you were a boy; keep clean; be tidy; don't show off; don't brag about yourself; don't be conceited; you have to/must/should (whatever)...

If no one comes forward with any positive messages then I write: I love you; you are adorable; you are perfect; you deserve

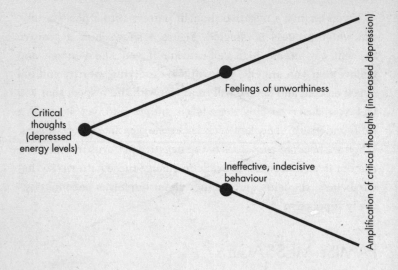

Figure 5 How our feelings and behaviour amplify our depressed energy

the best; you are creative; you are important.

When we grow up, we talk to ourselves in the same way that our parents talked to us. We use the same words and the same tone of voice to speak to ourselves because this is what we first learned to imitate. Listen to the tone of your inner voice. What sort of things do you say to yourself? Do you tell yourself how wonderful you are? Do you praise and support yourself? Do you love and value yourself? The self-loving voice is usually much too quiet to be heard; it is probably always silent. The voice inside which deafens everything else as it nags and condemns is a critical voice which is not supportive. All the critical statements which we have believed have become true for us in some way. Our beliefs create a self-fulfilling prophecy.

LOW SELF-OPINION → LOW EXPECTATIONS → POOR PERFORMANCE → I WAS RIGHT; I AM NO GOOD

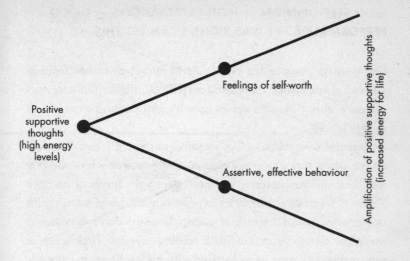

Figure 6 How our feelings and behaviour amplify our high energy

HIGH AND LOW ENERGY

Our critical thoughts create feelings and behaviour which reflect and amplify our low opinion of ourselves. Figure 5 shows how this happens.

Each time we criticize ourselves, the level of our energy drops. We literally 'depress' our energy. We all know what it feels like to be depressed; we lack clarity, motivation and zest. Who *cares* about making effective decisions when they feel like this? Who believes that they *could* ever make effective decisions when they feel like this? Such thoughts, feelings and behaviour are our negative patterns and they create low self-esteem.

The great news is that, now we have discovered the power of our beliefs, we can make that power work for us. Our critical thoughts create a self-fulfilling prophecy *and so do our positive thoughts.*

HIGH SELF-OPINION → HIGH EXPECTATIONS → GOOD PERFORMANCE → I WAS RIGHT; I CAN DO THIS

Our positive, supportive beliefs about ourselves create feelings and behaviour which reflect and amplify our high opinion of ourselves. Figure 6 demonstrates how we can lift and expand our energy levels.

Whenever we think well of ourselves our energy rises. Think of a time when you were very pleased with yourself – how did you feel, how did you behave, and how were your levels of energy? Whenever we talk to ourselves in positively affirming ways, we lift our energy. When I speak of energy levels, I don't necessarily mean the energy associated with aerobic exercise. High levels of physical energy *may* be associated with high self-esteem, but the energy I am talking about could be described as your energy for life, your zest and motivation: this energy is your life force, it is experienced internally and it makes you feel good! As you work through this book, you will learn to lift your energy as you change your negatively affirming patterns, which create low self-esteem and depression, into positively affirming patterns, which create high self-esteem and make you feel good.

EXERCISE:
Discovering Patterns

1 The ways I criticize myself
Make a list of all the ways you scold yourself:

....

....

You may have needed extra paper! We have such a lot to say about our inabilities and deficiencies.

2 The ways I encourage myself

Make a list of the things you say to yourself which are positive and supporting:

....

....

3 Childhood messages that I remember

Now use the 'brainstorming' technique to recall your own childhood messages. Just relax and let your ideas flow. Write down anything and everything that comes:

....

....

Now look at your answers to 1 and 2 and see how they relate to your answers to 3. How do the childhood messages that you remember affect the ways that you encourage or criticize yourself? Don't worry if you don't recognize a relationship between your answers. Patterns, especially negative ones, are often hidden very deeply within us. This book is full of techniques which will help you to unearth many family and cultural patterns which negatively affect your life and lower your self-esteem. This exercise serves only to highlight the important link between messages received in childhood and our messages to ourselves.

Did you have any answers to 2? If you did, that's great; if you didn't, you are one of the majority. Our critical voice is loud and scolding and it has a large (learned) vocabulary. Our encouraging voice has a small vocabulary (how many of your childhood messages were loving and encouraging?) and it is very timid.

Self-Encouragement and Parental Encouragement

We are extremely bashful about praising ourselves. It's OK to speak well of someone else, but it's not quite the thing to speak well of yourself, is it? You wouldn't want to be thought of as a person who 'blew their own trumpet', would you? We *all* suffer from this idea that self-encouragement is not 'nice'; it's showing off and is most unbecoming – especially for a girl. What a great example of a family pattern heavily influenced by a cultural pattern! If you are wondering if this pattern is one of yours, believe me, it is! It is a basic negative pattern which goes something like this: 'I am not really *that* good at anything and even if I was no one else would want to know and even if they did know they wouldn't like me for it and I want people to like me and approve of me because I really don't like myself very much because I am not really that good at anything...' Your personal variation on this theme may be slightly different, but if you are low in self-esteem it *will* include the need to address the ongoing problem of 'what other people will think'.

Sue is a high achiever with a well paid and interesting career. She has a small child, a supportive husband and a child-minder. She would appear to have everything and yet even she is low in self-esteem. How can this be when everything is working for her? A brilliant career, a wonderful family, plenty of money – however, none of these things in themselves create high self-esteem. Sue worked hard for her achievements, but she never felt satisfied with herself, and none of her accomplishments brought her fulfilment. Sue's main self-criticism was that she was never quite 'good enough'. She wasn't a 'good enough' mother because she worked; she wasn't 'good enough' at her job because of her family commitments; she could never give herself 100 per cent for her efforts. Her mother and father had always encouraged her to do well and Sue had plenty of support at home. She learned from her parents that 'you deserve to get whatever you want', and that 'women have the same rights as men'. These were the childhood messages which helped her to create her present lifestyle. These strong and powerful beliefs, however, were seriously undermined by another message which Sue internalized – 'be perfect'. Sue says that she was never actually told to 'be perfect', but that this message was always in the air. Sue understands that her parents did the very best they could to encourage her, but as they helped her to stretch her abilities so that she could achieve more, she actually began to feel that she could never succeed. Every time she achieved something new, there was never time to reward and appreciate her efforts. Her parents kept on moving the goal posts, so Sue never actually scored the goal and received the applause. The childhood messages which create our belief systems are not always spoken; many are to be found 'in the air'. These messages are subtle and extremely powerful and often very confusing.

REPEATING FAMILY PATTERNS

As a new-born baby your mind was clear. You had no preconceptions, no expectations, no limiting thoughts; nothing except excitement, a thirst for knowledge and the instinct to survive. In the first few years of your life you absorbed all stimuli at an enormous rate. Imagine that your senses are like a giant sponge which will soak up anything and everything without discretion. Your subconscious mind has no discriminating powers: it does not know what is 'true' or 'untrue', what is 'real' or 'not real'. It accepts everything literally. If, as a small child, you were told, 'You are beautiful and clever and I love you', you would believe this to be true. If you were told, 'You are stupid and no good', then you would believe this to be true. If you grew up with people who were unhappy and angry, then you would have absorbed many negative messages about yourself and the way the world works. These may have included such low self-esteem makers as: 'I'm no good', 'I make everyone unhappy', 'It's all my fault', 'It's bad to be angry'. Such beliefs create low self-worth and a miserable victim lifestyle. The messages we receive and absorb in our childhood create the life we have today.

Whatever our childhood background, we tend to re-create it in our adulthood, even if it was non-supportive. This may be hard to believe but it is true. Our early childhood years provide the basis for the rest of our lives. Whatever we learned becomes security to us; it is what we 'recognize'. There is a powerful incentive for us to attract and re-create negative patterns in our lives for two important reasons. Firstly, our known insecurities become securities to us, just because we know them. Secondly, each time we re-create a negative pattern, we provide ourselves with a chance to break that pattern.

Mary's father left when she was tiny and she was brought up by her mother who had a great distrust of men. Mary's relationships with men have been characterized by the following repeating patterns: needing a relationship with a man – repeating her childhood need for her father; clinging to the man – repeating her fear of abandonment by her father; choosing men who are bound to leave her – repeating her feelings of abandonment and lack of trust. And so Mary chose to have relationships which were bound to fail. After many broken relationships with men who just couldn't be what she wanted them to be (they just *wouldn't* change for her), she came to recognize the repeating nature of her own behaviour. The recognition of any negative pattern is very empowering because once we recognize that we are repeating behaviour which doesn't work for us we are back in the driving seat – we can act and *change* the pattern. Mary recognized that the men to whom she was attracted were no good for her; they were just helping her to re-create her abandonment/ lack of trust pattern and eventually she decided that she deserved more from her relationships. At the moment Mary is not involved in an intimate relationship and has not been for over a year. She says that she wants to get herself together and so has deliberately removed herself from the social whirl. In this way she is consciously breaking the pattern which involved the 'need' to have a man around. This has been hard for Mary because the negative patterns which we keep 'needing' to re-create are compulsive until we recognize them and change them. In moments of difficulty over the past year, Mary has had to resist the strong urge to find a man to lean on. She has been determined to stay alone so that she can get to know herself in a new way, and her self-esteem is increasing greatly as she has begun to break the back of her destructive pattern.

Later in this book we will be looking closely at the compulsive nature of our negative patterns. Thoughts, feelings and behaviours can be as addictive as any drug, but whenever we decide that it is time to break our addictions we become empowered to do so.

We are what we believe we are – we believe our thought, feeling and behaviour patterns. They are 'real' to us and ensure that our expectations for ourselves come true. When you are low in self-esteem, you are believing negative patterns. Your thoughts, feelings and behaviours reflect the belief that you are unworthy, no good, useless and undeserving. However, this belief is only 'real' for you if you allow it to be. Negative patterns are victim patterns. You are only a victim if you choose to be. Positive patterns are creative and are based on a belief that you are unique, talented and worthy, and that you deserve the best. Your family patterns become your patterns for life. If these patterns are positive, then your life will be an amazing and creative experience. If any of these patterns are negative, then you need to recognize them and change them so that you can realize your full human potential by becoming a woman with self-esteem.

2

Taking it Like a Woman – Cultural Patterns

The ways that we think, feel and behave are created by our own unique blend of learned family and cultural patterns. These two are usually interrelated and interdependent, but it is often possible to distinguish between their effects so that we can unravel the threads of our individual patterns and bring change into our lives. As women, we often become aware of our cultural conditioning before we understand the power of our family conditioning. As soon as we become conscious that our womanhood affects our status within society, the effect can be quite dramatic.

I was in my late twenties when I first became aware that my rights were limited because of my gender: it was the mid-1970s and feminism was on the rise. Now I find it incredible to believe that I took so long to see something that was so obvious. Nowadays the sexual debate begins in the classroom. Young women are becoming aware of their culturally prescribed roles and many are anxious to change a male-dominated power structure to give women the freedom to be what they want to be, to have equal status with men and to be given the respect they deserve. All women are entitled to these opportunities; they are a basic human right. Most women feel that they have to fight for these basic rights on an ongoing basis and that this battle is tiring, boring and incredibly confusing. The confusion arises because we don't really want to fight. If we are angered by an oppressive role, then it feels good to express that anger, but being oppressed and getting angry can develop into an ongoing cycle leading nowhere.

BLAME AND EMPOWERMENT

Women in groups eventually, and it seems inevitably, begin to discuss men. Women are fascinated, amazed, horrified, excited and revolted by men. These feelings are natural and are an expression of both our differences from, and our attraction to, the opposite sex. On the surface, it seems clear to us that our male-dominated culture undervalues women and that men are to blame. However, this line of thinking does not free or empower women in any way. Blaming men and yet wanting men creates internal chaos – anger, depression, resentment, guilt… *it does not create freedom.* Blaming is not a technique which will ever empower you. As soon as you blame you give away your power. If my feelings about myself depend upon the way that others treat me, then I am a victim. If you have power over me, then I have given you that power.

So what do we do if we find that our rights are limited because of our sex? First we need to recognize what is happening and then act in some way to change the situation. None of the women who have successfully fought for women's rights have been blamers – they have been activists. Blaming leads to low self-esteem and an inability to act effectively. Changes in society's attitude to women come about when the problem is recognized and when effective action is taken, not when women become stuck in recrimination.

The states of blame and empowerment are mutually exclusive. Every time I blame someone, I give that person some power over me. If it's 'all your fault' then only you can change the situation and I am just a helpless victim waiting for you to change. Figures 7a and 7b demonstrate the difference between blame and empowerment.

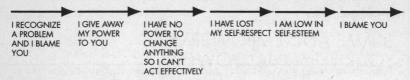

Figure 7a Blame as an ineffective tool for change

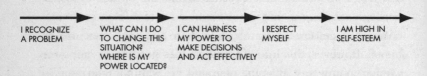

Figure 7b Empowerment as an effective tool for change

When we apply this concept of empowerment to real-life situations, we can see how the theory works at both a national and a domestic level. For example:

- The suffragettes mobilized their power and changed voting rights for women; women felt an increase in self-esteem and self-respect.
- Anne was physically abused by her husband for 15 years. She harnessed her power and left the relationship; she now respects herself and has increased her self-esteem.

Blame works for no woman. It sticks you in a puddle of glue from which there is no escape; blame and submission and low self-esteem go hand-in-hand.

I spent a number of years torturing the men in my life, torturing myself and feeling that I was getting absolutely nowhere with my personal emancipation. I felt angry a lot of the time; that was quite energizing, but it didn't seem to change my situation. I became divorced, but I didn't feel free. I didn't know how to harness my power because I didn't really know what or where my power was.

YOUR PERSONAL POWER

The concept of 'power' is often linked with ideas of struggle, authority and conflict, with an underlying understanding that one can only have power at the expense of another person. I use the word quite differently here.

Your power is your own. It belongs to you, and no one can change it, take it away or give you more. You create your own personal power or not, as the case may be. Self-empowerment is found in self-responsibility. If we blame other people or circumstances for what happens to us in our lives, then we hand over our power – we are saying, 'You are responsible and so only you can make my life better'. When we accept total responsibility for the quality of our lives, then we become empowered. However, taking responsibility for ourselves is sometimes very hard to do, especially when we are feeling low and vulnerable. Our inclination is to look outside ourselves to find something or someone to blame for our circumstances. Most of our cultural and family patterns are grounded in victim consciousness rather than creative consciousness. Were you taught that 'you create your own reality' or did you learn to blame 'them' (whoever 'they' may be) for whatever happened to you? These victim patterns run deep within us and we shall be unearthing them again and again as we move through this book. Victim patterns create low self-esteem – if it's someone else's fault, then I can't do anything to change the situation, I have lost my personal power (I have given it away to my victimizer).

Figure 8 demonstrates the ways in which we can allow our personal power to leak away, taking us from our highly focused centre, to beyond the boundaries of our personal power and into the realms of blame, disempowerment and low self-esteem. Here we begin to lose our sense of self-worth, we question our credibility and we begin to focus outside ourselves.

Look at the centre of Figure 8. Within the inner circle we experience our own personal power. We feel centred, balanced

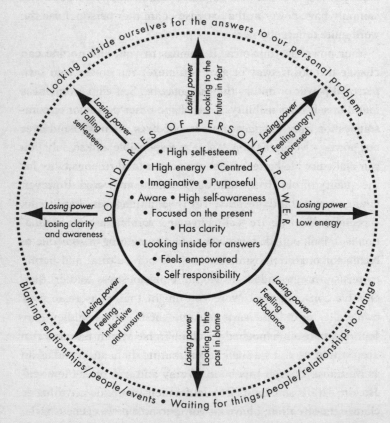

Figure 8 Losing personal power

and high in energy. We are focused in the present moment, we feel clear and decisive, and our actions are effective. The overall feeling is one of control with a clear understanding of our inner process and a sense of purpose. When we contact our personal power we are high in self-esteem. However, as we move from the very centre of the inner circle to the boundaries of our personal power, we begin to change our focus. At this boundary our self-esteem is threatened. This may occur for any reason and we all know only too well how quickly it can happen. If at this moment we try to alleviate our discomfort by beginning to look outwards, we are on a slippery slope towards becoming a victim and losing our inner focus and our personal power.

The arrows leading from the inner to the outer circle of Figure 8 demonstrate the feelings, thoughts and behaviour which are associated with allowing our power to leak away. As we look to blame an outside agency for our discomfort, we lose our sense of being in the present moment, and we may look to the past in blame or to the future in fear. We may feel angry and depressed as we lose our clarity and self-awareness. When we blame other people and events for our misfortunes we can only wait for others to change. If you ever find yourself doing this, you are looking in the wrong direction. The only way to change your circumstances is to change yourself, and the only way to change yourself is to develop your own personal power.

Rose is in her late forties and her children have just left home. She is married to Charles who works long hours as an accountant. Rose says that she is low in confidence because she no longer feels useful now that her children have gone. She says that she wants to try to find work, but that it will be 'impossible' for her because Charles wants her to stay and look after the home. He also says that there is no real financial need for her to work. So Rose stops thinking about going to work. (Because Charles needs looking after? Because the house needs looking after?

Because Charles must be obeyed?) Rose is losing power; she feels depressed, blames the past, fears the future and despises herself. Rose blames her family, and in particular her husband, for her circumstances. If only Charles wasn't so helpless, if only the house didn't need cleaning, if only I wasn't so depressed, if only I could do something, if only the children still lived at home, if only...

Eventually Rose is at her wits' end and she loses her temper with Charles, blaming him for her situation. Charles says that he never meant to stop her working and that he will do all he can to help around the house and to support Rose while she does what she wants to do. Rose gets even more depressed and doesn't try to find work. When Charles tries to talk to her about it, she screams that she is unskilled and too frightened to look for a job. At this point, Rose has turned back to focus on herself. Her real fears about work revolve around her own feelings of inadequacy and she has been using Charles as an excuse. Blame is a totally ineffective tool for change. Once Rose has put herself back in the centre, she becomes empowered. There is no one to blame for her situation and she is free to act. Although it is hard and a bit frightening, she enrols in a course at college and eventually finds a satisfying job in a home for children with special needs.

Whenever we find ourselves at the boundaries of our personal power, we feel sensitive and vulnerable. We begin to lose our personal power; it feels uncomfortable, we want to change this feeling and so we look at someone else, a relationship or an outside event to blame. As soon as we shift the focus, there is an immediate relief from the initial discomfort of loss of power. We start to feel better about ourselves as we blame someone else. However, this feeling cannot last, as it is not grounded in reality.

Victim consciousness is a state of mind which allows us not to take any responsibility for our lives. Listen to the conversations around you and hear this pattern being enacted at every moment of the day. People will blame everything and anybody for whatever is happening to them. 'I blame the politicians... It's all his/her fault... If only that hadn't happened... It will be all right when he changes... If only he would change... There's nothing I can do about it... If only it wasn't raining... If only it wasn't so hot...' – yes, we can even become victims to the weather! Listen to the way people talk, and become aware of your own victim status. There is no mileage in being a victim; it drains away all of your personal power. If you feel disempowered, then take the first step back to the powerful centre of your life by becoming conscious of what you are doing and how you are doing it. Become aware of your victim patterns, and then you can change them.

EXERCISE:
Losing Personal Power

Think of a time when you were feeling high in self-esteem and full of personal power and then suddenly the feeling changed. Maybe someone criticized you, or you thought they did, or you brought yourself down without anyone's help!

1 How did you feel when you were full of personal power?

....

....

....

2 How did you feel when the situation changed?

....

....

....

Look at Figure 8 on page 26. You are now at the boundaries of your personal power. However this happened, try to be aware of your reaction. Did you act immediately to retrieve your power by reminding yourself of your strong points or did you let your power leak away by becoming a victim to outside circumstances? If you gave your power away, how did you do it? Who or what did you blame and how did you feel?

3 I gave away my power by:

....

....

4 When I lost my power I felt:

....

....

It is highly likely that you gave your power away. Our strong victim patterns have been taught to us both by our families and by society. Both women and men suffer from these patterns, although women have learned a strong cultural imperative to become emotional victims to men. We will look at the implications of this cultural patterning in the second part of the book.

Whenever we allow our victim patterns to run our lives, we become disempowered. Self-awareness is the key to self-esteem. Remember that we have *learned* all of our thought, feeling and behaviour patterns, and that as soon as we become conscious of the patterns which create low self-esteem we can change them! If you have lost your personal power, then change your focus, stop looking at outside influences and look into yourself – for this is where your true power lies.

A WOMAN'S POWER

Our power as women is located in our freely flowing energy; creativity; self-awareness; excitement; intuition; thirst for life; tolerance; practicality; flexibility; emotionality; faith; desire; endurance; hope; appreciation and love. Our power lies within us and our potential is infinite. The realization of our true power lies in our quest for self-esteem. Are you experiencing your woman's power? Are you feeling creative, instinctive and wise, or are you feeling low and disempowered? If it is the latter, you are not alone; most women are not in touch with their most powerful abilities. We have learned many ways to limit our infinite potential. We have learned to create our own self-limiting behaviour and low self-expectations. For much of our lives, we women have felt undervalued, underestimated, underachieving and unsatisfied. We feel like this because we believe that we are powerless. However, *we are full of power and we can change the quality of our lives.*

There are no superwomen, only women who have learned to change their negative patterns. We belong to a long cultural tradition which has encouraged women to believe that men have the real power and women play a supportive, comforting and receptive role. Even as I write these words, I can feel my own and your own anger. However, blame will never resolve an issue. The truth is that we can never be *made* to feel like second-class citizens. We can never be *made* to feel anything.

Reclaiming personal power is always about focusing on your own beliefs, thoughts and actions. What are your deep beliefs about the differences between men and women? What did your mother believe about the roles of men and women in our society? What did your father feel about women? How did your father treat your mother? How did your mother treat your father? These are really deep and important questions for you to answer.

Even if you disagree with your parents' ideas about gender issues, their fundamental beliefs will have been internalized by you when you were too young to discriminate.

Before we can take effective action to educate others to treat women and men with equal respect, we must look closely at the patterns we ourselves learned about the relationships between men and women. I am sometimes astounded by my own self-invalidating patterns in this area. I have worked so hard on my self-esteem, and yet I can still find myself feeling intimidated, angry or confused by someone *just because he is a man*. This is not an easy thing to admit, but it helps to clarify the powerful nature of our deep patterning. It also helps me to resolve another problem which I find equally astounding and which is even harder to admit. As I work to affirm the roles of women positively within our society, I encounter great resistance – *from women!* As I discuss the ideas in this book with other people, I hear so many put-downs of women *by women* that I am almost too embarrassed to admit it. I wasn't expecting this sort of reaction and I have spent a long time thinking about what it all means. Of course, the answer is very simple and lies way back where we began the discussion of family and cultural patterning. However politically correct we have become, however intellectually aware we are, we can never, never overcome the deep belief structure that we learned in our babyhood unless we become conscious of these deep patterns and then actively change them.

EXERCISE:

What Are Your Deep Beliefs About Women and Men?

What did you learn about the roles of women and men when you were lying in your pram?

1 What did your mother believe to be her role in society?

....

....

2 What did your father believe to be his role in society?

....

....

3 Did these beliefs affect the ways in which your parents treated each other?   **Yes/No**

4 How did your mother treat your father?

....

....

5 How did your father treat your mother?

....

....

6 Can you see any connection between your parents' attitude to gender issues and your own?

....

....

Sometimes these links are very deep and only emerge as we continue to work on our own personal patterning.

BALANCING ENERGY

We are empowered when we are high in self-esteem and we are high in self-esteem when our energies are balanced. Look back at Figures 1 and 2 on pages 2 and 5. Whether we are female or male, the quality of our life experiences is measured by the degree of balance in our lives. We are more than our physical selves. To every moment of our lives we bring our whole selves: mind, body, spirit and emotions. Our high self-esteem depends upon the interrelationship between our mental, physical, emotional and spiritual energies. If our energy is blocked in any one of these areas, then our whole experience is affected. Imagine that we have just met. We are engaged in conversation and we are both feeling good, our energy is flowing freely and we are high in self-esteem. You then say something and I feel angry as a result of what you have said. Instead of communicating my feelings to you, I try to hide them away. I have blocked my emotional energy and my whole experience will now be affected. My self-esteem will fall because my energy is now out of balance.

Life is all about the interaction of different types of energy. You have your energy, I have mine and we affect each other and create new energy between us. I like this simple way to describe our relationships; it is very meaningful and offers great insights. Ancient Chinese philosophy states that our human consciousness has two opposite but complementary parts. This is called the Yin–Yang principle and is demonstrated in Figure 9 which shows a symmetrical relationship between the Yin (female, dark, receptive) and the Yang (male, light, creative). Human energy comprises the Yin and the Yang in a relationship which is ever moving. When either of the male or female forces reaches the extreme, it already has within it the seed of its opposite. We all have both male and female characteristics, regardless of whether we are women or men. This ancient philosophy has been

Figure 9 Yin and Yang

embraced by western psychology and this way of looking at our sexuality provides an empowering tool.

Figure 2 on page 5 shows how our male and female energies come together to create our experiences. Our spiritual and emotional energies belong to our femaleness, while our mental and physical energies belong to our maleness. The key to empowerment and high self-esteem for all women and men lies in our ability to balance our own male and female energies. When mind and body (male energy) and spirit and emotion (female energy) are balanced, our energy flows freely and our experience is harmonious, creative and high in self-esteem. When our energy is blocked anywhere in this cycle, our spiritual, mental, emotional and physical parts will not be balanced – in other words, our male and female energies will be out of balance. Look at the two separate and yet supporting parts which represent the totality of your energy in Figure 10.

Inner Male and Inner Female Energies

Our inner female represents our inspirational energy; she receives our instinctive 'knowingness' about things, our gut feelings, our intuition. She is all-wise and all-knowing, and is the channel for our spiritual connection with the universal energy.

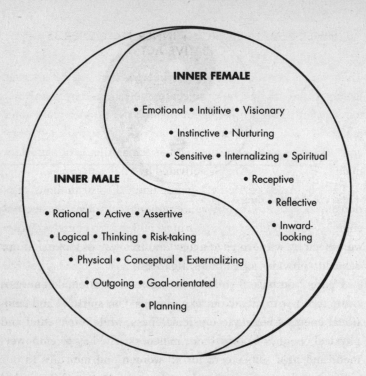

INNER FEMALE

- Emotional • Intuitive • Visionary
- Instinctive • Nurturing
- Sensitive • Internalizing • Spiritual
- Receptive
- Reflective
- Inward-looking

INNER MALE

- Rational • Active • Assertive
- Logical • Thinking • Risk-taking
- Physical • Conceptual • Externalizing
- Outgoing • Goal-orientated
- Planning

Figure 10 Inner female and inner male energy

This spirituality is expressed in our feelings and needs. If we trust the messages of our inner female, we can put our inner male to work to externalize her wisdom. Our inner male represents our active principle. He is the part of us that goes out into the world and makes things happen. If our inner male and inner female do not work in harmony with each other, our energy will be out of balance and we will be low in self-esteem. This is true for both women and men. When our inner female and inner male energies are balanced, we listen to the intuitive awareness of our female energy and then utilize our male energy to create effective and decisive behaviour. We are involved in the creative process every moment of our lives.

INNER FEMALE ENERGY + INNER MALE ENERGY →
CREATIVE ACT

This process is really very simple. Imagine that you get a strong feeling to embark on a new project (communicated by your inner female) and then you set about making the project real (inner male in action). Your intention is prompted by your spiritual/emotional awareness (inner female) and the decision-making and action-taking is activated by your inner male.

The quality of our lives depends upon the harmonious relationship between our spiritual, emotional, physical and mental energies or, in other words, our male and female energies. When we are low in self-esteem, we need to discover where our energy is blocked. Look at Figure 10. Do you relate to one half of the diagram more than the other? Are some aspects of your energy more developed than others? Where is your energy strong? Where is your energy flagging?

EXERCISE:
Creating Your Own Reality

Is your energy balanced? Are you high or low in self-esteem? What sort of reality are you creating for yourself?

Think of a personal success story. How did you create this reality?

1 The success story was:

....

....

2 What were the feelings associated with the beginning of the project? Did you listen to these feelings?

....

....

3 How did you activate the project?

....

....

Now think of something which did not become a success for you. Work through the exercise again and answer Questions 1 to 3 in relation to an unsuccessful project. Did you listen to your gut feelings? Did you follow your instincts? Did you trust your inner awareness? Was your action-taking focused and decisive and did it reflect your feelings? In other words, did your inner male and inner female energies support each other?

Imbalanced Energy

Culturally, we have not been taught to understand our energy in terms of mutually supportive male and female aspects. In our society thought and action are high status activities, whereas spiritual and emotional awareness are given no priority. We have learned that proactive (male) energy is all-important and that emotional and spiritual awareness should be controlled and even denied. Individually, we have learned to put our inner male energies in charge, so that thought, planning and logic override our instinctive messages. Both women and men have largely denied their female power and have put their inner male in the driving seat. This inner lack of balance has been reflected culturally so that our society has traditionally been male-dominated with women in a submissive role.

Because we have not learned to view our energy as a mixture of male and female, we have been inclined to associate male energy with men and female energy with women. In this way, women have become the *symbols* of female energy – nurturing, receptive, sensitive and inward-looking – and have lost their ability to act assertively in the world. Similarly, men have come to symbolize male energy – logical, conceptual, assertive and outward-looking – and have lost their emotional and intuitive awareness. Balance is the key. We do not need to be dependent upon men; we can develop our own male energy and learn to take care of ourselves. We do not need to provide round-the-clock nurturing and emotional support for the men in our lives; they can develop their own female energy and learn to take care of themselves spiritually and emotionally. When men and women can balance their own energies, they can come together in a relationship which is not needy but is based on mutual respect and self-esteem.

Times are changing and women are learning to express themselves effectively in the world by acknowledging and trusting their female energy while learning to develop and activate their male energy. We are questioning the validity of traditional cultural expectations based on men internalizing and expressing only male energy and women internalizing and expressing only female energy. We can change the powerful negative conditioning which we have learned. The following questionnaire will help you see where your energy needs balancing.

QUESTIONNAIRE:
How Balanced Is Your Energy?   **Yes / No**

1 I listen to my gut reaction.
2 Sometimes I am ruled by my emotions.
3 I am afraid to take chances.
4 I find it hard to put my ideas into practice.
5 I often hide my feelings.
6 I trust my intuition and act upon it.
7 I need a man in my life.

8 I respect myself.

9 I get confused easily.

10 I am in a poor relationship at the moment.

11 Iam enjoying my life.

12 I am sometimes a victim.

13 I am good at planning and achieving my goals.

14 I have no goals.

15 I have secrets which I am afraid to share.

16 I deserve a happy and successful life.

17 I sometimes hate men.

18 I am a strong and powerful woman.

19 The men in my life treat me with respect.

20 The men in my life treat me badly.

21 I am decisive.

22 I need to look after people.

23 I have relationships with people who are not good for me.

Reflect on your answers; they demonstrate the thought, feeling and behaviour patterns which run your life. Where do your patterns support your self-esteem and where do they not? How do your victim patterns express themselves? What beliefs have you internalized about the roles played by men and women? Are your energies balanced? Do you need to develop your female energy? Do you need to develop your male energy? Where is your energy strong and where is it weak?

You can change your life and create high self-esteem by changing the negative patterns which do not work for you. This book will help you to discover the precise nature of your limiting patterns. Discover your personal power by taking responsibility for all that happens in your life. One way of recognizing how you create your own reality is by looking at the interplay of your male and female energies.

Becoming Aware – Changing Our Patterns

*La distance n'y fait rien;
il n'y a que le premier pas qui coûte.*

(The distance doesn't matter;

it is only the first step that is difficult.)

(MARQUISE DU DEFFAND)

Our individual blend of cultural and family patterning creates the unique fabric of our lives. In some places the material will be strong and durable; in others it will be weak and falling apart. Some parts may be extremely beautiful and others dark and gloomy. We can colour and strengthen the fabric of our lives as soon as we become aware of our creative capacity. When we understand *how* we create our own reality, we can change the quality of our life experiences.

EXERCISE:

The First Step to Change

Consider an area of your life where you are experiencing difficulties.

1 Briefly describe the problem:

....

....

2 What would you like to change about this situation?

....

....

3 Describe the new ideal situation:

....

....

What part have you played in helping to create this problem? This may be difficult to see. The following questions might prove helpful. Have I allowed someone to treat me badly? Have I been honest with myself about my true feelings? Have I let my feelings be known to others?

4 I have helped to create this problem by:

....

....

What is the *first step* that you would need to take to begin to change the present situation? This first step will be very small but may feel very difficult to take. Do you need to change your attitude or beliefs in some way? Are you not saying something that you need to say? Are you protecting someone? Are you ashamed of something? Are you afraid of the consequences of taking this step? Be brave and be honest with yourself here. There is no need to promise action; the need is just to recognize and to state whatever your first step might be.

5 My first step would be to:

....

....

EFFECTING CHANGE

Life can sometimes feel very hard to bear. Unforeseen circumstances occur and we find ourselves lost in a sea of conflicting emotions, unable to make clear decisions and incapable of positive action. Such a situation can feel very alarming and disempowering if it brings about a loss of self-esteem and a loss of control of the circumstances. At this stage we feel like helpless victims and may well find ourselves looking for someone or something to blame. We have seen how blaming supports our victim status by ensuring that we take no responsibility for our life events. And so we may sit in blame and inactivity and depression and anger and low self-esteem... until a magic moment comes when we feel ready to change our situation in some way.

It is truly amazing and wonderful to see the power of women to rise up amidst extremes of adversity and emotional pain and to find within themselves the strength to take charge of their lives once again. That powerful, instinctive, creative and enduring energy of women wins through again and again. We can always change our lives, we can always pick up the pieces and create a new scenario. When that moment comes when we just cannot 'sit there' any longer, then we are ready to discover the exact nature of the first step to recovery from our helplessness. This step is always the hardest because it is the step that we have been too afraid to take all along. There is always a fear accompanying great change; our habitual patterns are comfortable, even when they no longer work for us.

The previous exercise was designed to promote an awareness of a necessary first step for you. As soon as you recognize the part that you have played in the making of this problematic situation, you will know whatever it is that you first need to do to resolve the difficulties. This step will involve changing your thought, feeling and behaviour patterns in some way.

The Five-Step Programme for Change

There are five major steps that need to be taken in order to bring about change. They are:

- Assess the situation.
- Decide what you would like to change.
- Specify your preferred outcome.
- Recognize the negative patterning involved.
- Change the negative patterns – re-pattern your life.

Becoming aware and changing our patterns requires all the support we can gather. Part 2 of this book demonstrates the practical application of the Five-Step Programme for Change using a supportive network which I call Techniques for Change.

TECHNIQUES FOR CHANGE

These techniques for change include affirmations, creative visualization, forgiveness, balancing your energy and self-appreciation. You may have heard of some of these methods and may even have used them. They are all powerful tools which work all the more efficiently if you know exactly how to operate them. All of these techniques are grounded in a strong theoretical base;

there are exact and precise reasons why they work and if you understand the theory the tools become more effective.

Affirmations

Affirmations are any statements that we make. These obviously include all spoken communications and they may have negative or positive associations. Our spoken statements are created by our thoughts. Try to imagine what sort of thoughts might have created the following statements:

- What a stupid fool I am.
- I really enjoy your company.
- I'm always clumsy.
- Life is a struggle.
- People are fascinating.

It has been estimated that we process about 50,000 thoughts in one day. Can you even begin to remember 100 of the thoughts which you have had today? Has this thinking been positively supporting or negatively undermining? Self-respectful and self-supporting thoughts come from self-belief. If you are high in self-esteem, you will believe in yourself and so your thoughts and spoken statements about yourself will be positive affirmations. Every thought that you have is an affirmation which can have a negative or a positive effect. If you are low in self-belief, then your thoughts about yourself will be negative. If you are thinking badly about yourself, you will feel worthless. Your behaviour will be unfocused and indecisive because it will reflect these feelings.

There is an incredible amount of private chatter going on within our heads. Next time you are with a group of people, reflect for a moment on the amount of internal dialogue that everyone is experiencing while they are *simultaneously* involved in external dialogue. The speech reflects the thoughts; the external reflects the internal. We are truly talking to ourselves all of the time. The quality of this inner experience depends entirely upon the nature of our beliefs.

We are inclined to identify closely with our beliefs because we think that we have made rational decisions about what to believe and what not to believe. What exactly do you believe to be true about yourself?

EXERCISE:
Your Self-Belief

Look at this list. Which phrases do you think describe you best? Which phrases would you say least describe you?

- Thoughtful and kind
- Able to express my feelings
- Boring
- Creative
- Articulate and clever
- Able to communicate well with others
- Good at making decisions
- Not at all creative
- Good at reasoning
- Basically a lazy person
- Interesting
- Not really good at anything in particular
- Well motivated and energetic
- Not very clever
- Good at coping with any situation
- Inclined to give up easily
- Able to tackle new projects
- Not good enough at certain things
- Deserving the best that life has to offer me

Consider your answers. Do your beliefs about yourself serve to increase or decrease your feelings of self-worth? Why do you believe things which lower your self-esteem? Look closely at the beliefs which have a negative effect on your life – are they really true? We are all inclined to find fault with ourselves and to believe that in some way or another we really are not quite good enough. But for whom or for what are you not quite good enough?

Acquiring Basic Beliefs

Think back to your babyhood. Imagine yourself sitting in your pram. See this tiny little girl taking her first steps. See her smiling and playing with her toys. Was she good enough? Was she less than perfect? When did she change? How did she change? This beautiful baby girl hasn't gone anywhere; she is still a part of you.

For the first few years of your life, your mind was an open book with blank pages. Your open-mindedness ensured that you believed everything that you learned. Without the capacity to filter the incoming information, the baby girl within you accepted unquestioningly all the verbal and non-verbal messages that she received. By the time you were about three years old, your book of basic beliefs about the way you and your world work was full. Of course, you have changed as you have grown. You have learned many things since the age of three but your basic beliefs will not have changed unless you have been consciously changing them. If you describe yourself as stupid, lazy, too fat/thin/ugly, useless, worthless, pathetic, incapable, boring etc, you can be sure that these words or the meaning behind these words is part of your basic belief structure, written in that open book of your babyhood. If you were criticized in your childhood, then you will not only believe these criticisms to be true, but you will also re-create these critical relationships in your adulthood. Old comfortable patterns can be so dangerous for us. What can we do about these basic beliefs? Is it worth trying to do anything? Are you fulfilling your unique potential? Is your life purposeful and meaningful? Are you creating the reality that you desire? Are you high in self-esteem?

If you have answered 'no' to any of these questions, then you are missing out on the gift of your life. You are truly an amazing, incredible and unique person and you only need to believe it. You are what you believe you are. What do you believe you are?

EXERCISE:
You Are What You Believe You Are

Write down 20 words which describe you.

1	2
3	4
5	6
7	8
9	10
11	12
13	14
15	16
17	18
19	20

Look at your answers one at a time and decide which beliefs have positive implications for you and which have negative associations. Put an N or a P next to each word. Now go back and consider each of your N answers. Think carefully about why you believe these things to be true. Ask yourself each time if this is really true. You may even get a feeling about *why* you believe a negative thought about yourself.

Changing Basic Beliefs

Beliefs are only thoughts that we think are true. Thoughts can always be changed. If we learned to believe things that are non-supportive, then we can exchange these beliefs for new ones which are encouraging and confidence-building. We can change our basic beliefs by making positive affirmations about ourselves and our world.

Those of you who are familiar with the concepts of self-belief and affirmations may feel that you are just covering old ground. However, I think that it is vitally important that we all look again at the reasoning behind the use of affirmations. Our basic beliefs create the quality of our lives. We create exactly what we believe we deserve. Our statements of belief (spoken and unspoken) can create an amazing life experience.

The concept of consciously changing the quality of our lives by making positive affirmations is sometimes hard for people to take on board. How can it be so simple? How can I possibly change my life by saying 'I love and value myself'? Many people that I meet on workshops admit that they have great reservations about the effective use of affirmations. There is a lot of talk nowadays about 'being positive', but often the psychological theory supporting the use of affirmations has not been explained. It really is so simple and so profound.

Look back at the exercise 'Your Self-Belief' on page 46, and choose a negative statement which you used to describe yourself. Suppose I believe that I am not at all creative. How do I perpetuate and indeed amplify~ this belief? Look at Figure 5 on page 14. 'I am not at all creative' is the critical thought. The feelings associated with this belief are powerlessness and the behaviour linked with the belief will be characterized by helplessness – and so I amplify the effects of my critical thought and become a victim (see Figure 11).

EXERCISE:

How You Amplify Your Negativity

1 Look at Figure 12 and insert one of your own negative statements taken from the exercise 'Your Self-Belief' on page 46. This statement is your critical thought.
2 Now repeat this negative statement to yourself and simultaneously *be aware* of the feelings which come along with this belief.
3 Name the most dominant feelings and insert them in the diagram.
4 How do you act when you are feeling this way? Describe your behaviour and complete the diagram.

Effects of Negative and Positive Thought

And so from one small negative thought we create matching feelings and behaviours which support and amplify that negativity. Listen to the ways in which people talk about others and about themselves. Be aware of the effects of any negatively charged statements. We can change our lives by changing our basic beliefs. We can change our basic beliefs by making positive affirmations about ourselves. Once we have discovered a belief which doesn't work for us, we can contradict this belief.

Let's go back to Figure 5 and look again at the statement 'I am not at all creative'. Imagine that I believe this to be true. The first question to ask is whether this belief works for me. What this belief does is to ensure inactivity and non-creativity. Figure 11 demonstrates a self-fulfilling prophecy. I believe that I am not creative and my feelings and behaviour will support and enhance this belief. We create self-fulfilling prophecies in this way.

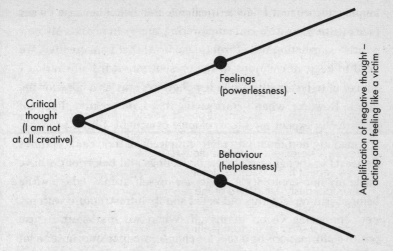

Figure 11 How our negative affirmations create our feelings and behaviour and so amplify our negativity

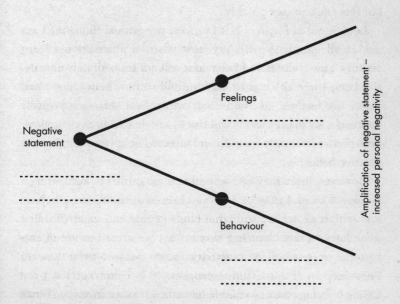

Figure 12 The amplification of your negative affirmations

Let us imagine that I decide to change this belief because I want to create new positive and empowering energy in my life. My new positive affirmation will affirm (make firm) that I am creative. We need to keep affirmations in the present tense. If I affirm that I am *going* to be creative, then it will always stay as a hope for the future. However, when I start saying that I *am* creative, I cannot realistically expect my life to change overnight. I have probably affirmed my non-creativity many hundreds of thousands of times (at least) in thoughts, statements, feelings and behaviour. I have made my non-creativity a reality for myself. It may take a while before I can replace this old belief and its infrastructure with my new energizing vision of myself. When we first start to use positive affirmations as a tool for change, we may encounter a lot of internal resistance. The new belief contradicts the old belief, and before we mentally exchange new for old, we may experience some inner confusion. It is quite natural to feel this way initially, but this stage passes quickly.

Look again at Figure 12. If I replace my critical thought ('I am not at all creative') with my new positive affirmation ('I am creative') my feelings and behaviour will not immediately change. However, when the transition from old to new belief has taken place, my feelings and behaviour will reflect this new positive approach. My energy levels will rise as my new feelings of empowerment and my newly focused and directed behaviour amplify my positive belief.

However, there may be something to be gained by remaining a helpless victim. I may be involved in a pattern of victim behaviour which allows me to blame other people and ensures that I don't have to risk changing in any way. We are all aware of this pattern; we have all been there at some point. Maybe you are knee-deep in this pattern right now. It is characterized by a feeling of being stuck (someone described it as wearing lead boots in a puddle of treacle). If you are wearing lead boots at the moment, you will also feel low in self-esteem and will feel cynical and doubtful about the power of positive affirmations. The quality of your own experience is the only way to test for the truth. Part 2 of this book will provide plenty of opportunity to test the theory behind changing basic beliefs by making positive affirmations. Give it a try and see if the theory works in practice. There is nothing to lose and everything to gain.

Creative Visualization

We create the quality of our lives by the quality of our thoughts. However, our thoughts don't stand alone; they are accompanied by our mental pictures. What sort of images of yourself do you project into the universe?

Relax and close your eyes – how do you see yourself? You may not actually *see* anything, but you will experience something, an awareness of your imagination at work. Your imagination is your most powerful creative tool, but it is often severely underestimated. Most of us have been taught to believe that our imagination is not 'real', but the truth is that we actually create our lives using our belief system and our imagination. It might seem hard to believe, but you are in charge of the creative process of your life.

Think of something simple which you are fairly sure that you are going to receive. You have positive expectations that you will receive it, positive pictures of yourself getting it, and no worries about not having it – and so your actions are successfully directed to make your wish come true. Everything was once a thought and a vision in someone's mind. Your house, your car, your clothes, your food – all began as an idea and a vision.

When you next make a meal, reflect on the process of how it came together. You felt hungry, you decided to make dinner, you imagined what you would make (with thoughts and pictures) and then you took the necessary actions *knowing* that you could make the meal a reality. We follow this simple process every time we create something. Perhaps the key to the process lies in the *knowing* that we can achieve our aim. It is far easier to know that we can create beans on toast than it is to know that we can realize a great ambition. However, the process is the same and the requirements are always positive thoughts, feelings and pictures which then produce focused and decisive action.

Great inventions, new ideas and wonderful art and music are created in exactly the same way. For example, Beethoven, Marie Curie, Michelangelo and Nelson Mandela all used their desire, vision and belief to create their marvellous achievements.

EXERCISE:
Creating Your Own Reality

Think about a situation where you really wanted something and you got it. Now relax and close your eyes and remember the thoughts, feelings and behaviour which were linked with your success.

1 **The thing I wanted:**

....

2 **The thoughts I had before I received it:**

....

3 **The feelings I had about receiving it:**

....

4 **The actions I took in order to get it:**

....

5 **The thoughts I had after I received it:**

....

6 The feelings I had after I had received it:

....

The process of consciously creating our own reality always requires strong and powerful thoughts and pictures which derive from a precise intention and highly motivated desire. Perhaps you don't feel that you can find this sort of commitment within you. Maybe you have no specific outcomes in mind. This conscious focus does not require special strength – in fact, we use more energy when we are unconsciously creative. We are always in the process of creating our lives. Every thought, picture, feeling and action comes together to create our life experience. We make things happen and the quality of the 'happening' depends entirely on what we expect for ourselves, how we see it happening and, at the deepest level, what we actually believe we deserve.

Go through the exercise again in relation to a situation where you did *not* get what you wanted. After you have done the exercise, answer the following questions.

- How much did you really want it?
- Did you believe that it was within your grasp?
- Did you imagine yourself having it?
- Did you think that you deserved it?
- Were you highly motivated?
- Were you decisive and assertive and realistic?

Can you detect any reasons why you didn't reach your goal?

If you really put your heart into something, gave it your best shot and it still didn't happen, then that particular reality was not right for you at that time. We create what we can handle, but sometimes we may try to overshoot the mark.

The way we see ourself forms an important part of the creative process. Self-critical thoughts and images create low self-esteem.

We create new and improved realities for ourselves by making positive affirmations and by visualizing ourselves acting out these affirmations.

EXERCISE:

Creating New Realities

Read each of the following affirmations and simultaneously visualize them becoming true for you.

- I am a strong and powerful woman.
- I am intelligent and resourceful.
- I trust my intuition.
- I love being a woman.
- I am assertive.
- My body is beautiful.
- I am always doing the best I can.
- I enjoy sex.
- My relationships are supportive.
- I can be independent.
- I create my own reality.
- I can have what I want.
- I am decisive.
- I am good at expressing my feelings.
- I can rely on myself.

As you say each of these affirmations, you may feel that they are not true. They may not be true for you now, but you can make them become true. Connect your images with your thoughts, and *see* yourself living out these affirmations. Create mental scenes where you are actually being assertive; enjoying sex; having what you want; being intelligent and resourceful etc. Use your imagination; it is such a powerful resource.

If you don't talk happy,
And you never have a dream,
Then you'll never have a dream come true.

(TAKEN FROM *SOUTH PACIFIC*)

Forgiveness

Forgiveness means giving up, letting go.

(LOUISE HAY, *LOVE YOURSELF
HEAL YOUR LIFE WORKBOOK*)

As we work on our old patterning, by using affirmations and creative visualization, we will probably discover some of the roots of our negative beliefs and expectations. We may be able to link our negativity with certain childhood messages that we received from our parents, caretakers, teachers, siblings etc. At this stage it is easy to start blaming those who took care of us. Remember two things:

- People can only teach what they know and understand themselves. Your parents did the best they could.
- Blame is an ineffective tool for change. Harness your power, release the blame and you will move forward in your own development.

Whenever I introduce forgiveness as a tool for change, I encounter opposition. How can forgiving someone else have anything to do with my own development? Why should I forgive him when what he did to me is totally unpardonable? I will never forget what she did; the pain is always with me; I can never forgive her. I feel so angry, so how can I forgive and why should I? What good will it do me? I will hate him forever and he deserves it.

Denise is 35. She is unmarried and is an only child. She was sexually abused by her father from the age of eight until she was 14. Her mother 'turned a blind eye' to the goings-on and Denise herself has only just begun to admit to the abuse. Her mistrust of her parents and her sense of shame created a pattern of abusive relationships for Denise. She believed that she was worthless and always to blame and so was a victim with low self-esteem in every area of her life. She attracted people into her life who were no good for her. This confirmed her belief that she didn't deserve anything better.

These are the bare bones of her pattern of victim consciousness. Denise was an alcoholic and it was the 'coming out' in this area that eventually revealed the abuse. The story was complex and the problems were many. At present, Denise has not had an intimate relationship for three years and has not drunk alcohol for over two years. She has been dealing with the issue of accepting that she was a victim of sexual abuse by her father with her mother's silent allowance. Denise wanted to tell her story because the whole issue for her at the moment revolves around this question of forgiveness.

D: I am so angry most of the time, and when I'm not angry I'm flat and depressed with no energy and life feels empty.

Me: How do you feel about your parents at the moment?

D: I hate them, but I still want their approval. They say I'm making it all up and that there is something wrong with me. But I know it's true and that they are lying. Sometimes I feel like I'm going crazy. If it wasn't for the others [a support group for the sexually abused], I think I would go off the wall.

Me: What is the main difficulty facing you now?

D: Dealing with my incredibly powerful rage and confusion. For all of those years [of denial] I was a very unemotional person. I didn't have many feelings and so I didn't have to deal with them. And now it feels like I'm making up for lost time. To start with, when I first admitted to myself and to you and the others [support group] that I had been sexually abused, I was really strong and I think that my rage made me strong.

Me: Does your rage still help you to feel strong?

D: No, it doesn't work like that any more. I just feel worn out with anger and I don't know where to put it [the anger]. I feel guilty about my feelings of hate and I'm confused and I don't know what to do.

Denise and I went on to discuss the concept of forgiveness. She said that someone had talked about forgiveness at the very beginning (when she first discussed her abuse) and that she had gone 'absolutely mad' with them.

D: I said, 'How dare you say that to me! They are to blame and I can never forgive the way that they have taken my life away from me.' And I had to feel like that at first, but now it doesn't work if I keep thinking in that way.

Me: What do you mean when you say 'It doesn't work'?

D: I needed to feel so angry at first because that was what kept me going. At least I could respect myself for being honest in that way. But now I've expressed a lot of rage and if I keep on doing it now, I feel like I'm just going round and round in circles and not moving on. I've got to be able to let go of all this so that I can start to build a new life for myself.

Forgiveness is a creative act. It does not mean letting anyone get away with anything – it means exactly the opposite. Forgiveness means letting go of all feelings that tie you to the person who wronged you. To forgive means to look closely at what happened and to accept that it happened. We cannot let go of anything until we can accept it. The second stage requires that we acknowledge all those feelings connected with the wrongdoing. Don't be afraid of your feelings. They cannot hurt you; only denied feelings create hurt. And when we reach the third stage, we can start to contemplate the meaning of forgiveness. This is the stage that Denise had reached when she said that she wasn't 'moving on'.

Forgiveness is indeed a creative act that actually begins when we are ready to look closely at the misdeed. The process continues when we allow ourselves to feel all of our rage. We cannot let go of our feelings until we have experienced them. So even at this stage, when Denise said that she could 'never forgive' her parents, she was *already* involved in the process of forgiveness. By the time we are ready to start to think about letting go of our blame and hatred, we are actually well into the forgiveness process.

Stage three is the easy bit; it's the getting to this stage that is most painful. Once we are ready to forgive, we can formulate our own personal forgiveness strategy. This allows for all situations and any eventuality. This may be a part forgiveness for now or until the next time; it could be a total pardon or a forgiveness for part of the offence; you could give one more chance or lots of chances or a conditional chance. You make the rules and all of the decisions.

You know when you have forgiven because you feel lighter; you have nothing much to say about the issue; you don't want anything and there is nothing left to wait for. You are free to leave your pain!

Balancing Your Energy

Any time you release a belief, change a goal,
or develop different expectations, you will
automatically change your future.

(SANAYA ROMAN AND DUANE PACKER,
OPENING TO CHANNEL)

You can choose to create victim consciousness and low self-esteem for yourself or you can create a powerful and purposeful future. The choice is always yours. What have you been choosing?

We create new realities by changing our physical, emotional, mental and spiritual patterns. To realize our innate potential, we need to balance all of our energies. Figure 1 on page 2 shows us how every moment of our lives is an expression of the coming together of our spiritual, mental, emotional and physical energy.

As you are reading, consider the energies which you bring to this experience. You are engaging all of your awareness, you bring your whole self and integrate all of your faculties. You are having a spiritual experience of your own inner awareness. This is your *connection* with the life force. You are *understanding* with your mental energy; having *feelings* via your emotional energy and being *active* by using your physical energy. Figure 13 shows how each 'type' of energy accesses a different 'type' of experience.

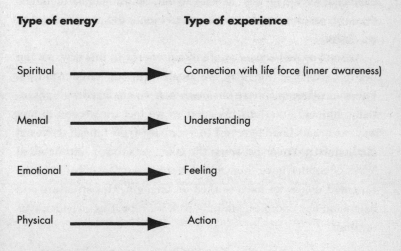

Type of energy	Type of experience
Spiritual	Connection with life force (inner awareness)
Mental	Understanding
Emotional	Feeling
Physical	Action

Figure 13 Energy levels and experience

When we combine the 'types' of energy which we use at each level of our being we are able to have a whole, well balanced experience. Our spiritual, mental, emotional and physical elements are interactive; they affect each other and are mutually dependent. When I speak of 'levels' I am only talking about the different ways which we have of experiencing. We are able to connect, feel, understand and act. The experience of interaction is multi-dimensional.

(LYNDA FIELD, *CREATING SELF-ESTEEM*)

This way of looking at our experiences as energetic interactions gives a whole new perspective to our lives. If our energies are not balanced, our experience will be low in self-esteem; we will feel low in energy, depressed and victimized. If our energies are balanced, we will be high in self-esteem; we will feel harmonious, decisive, assertive and empowered to create the personal reality we desire.

As soon as we become aware of our energy in this way, we can begin to change the way we deal with our circumstances. Imbalances become more obvious when we are faced with potentially difficult situations. As soon as we feel threatened in any way, we are inclined to revert to 'type'. By 'type' I mean the usual method we use to 'cope' when the going gets rough. Our habitual 'ways of coping' have their foundations in our basic belief structure, and unless we have worked on changing this structure and balancing our energies, we may well be repeating negative patterning.

What Type of Person Do You Think You Are?

Of course, we are all whole. We all experience spiritual, mental, emotional and physical energy. You may feel that you always achieve a good balanced 'mix' of these energies during your interactions. If you do, then you are a person who is extremely flexible, consciously creative and high in self-esteem. Most of us do not feel like this all of the time because our energies are out of balance.

Look at the characteristics below and tick any of those in each section which describe you. Score 1 for each tick.

Spiritual (Energy = Connecting)

- Enjoys looking inward, is self-reflective and aware of the subtler levels of vibration.
- Uses relaxation techniques, possibly interested in yoga, t'ai chi or breathing exercises.
- Aware of diet, may be a vegetarian.
- Interested in alternative therapies, healing, channeling.
- Interested in religion.
- Enjoys peace and quiet, might live or want to live in the country.
- Strong awareness of planetary problems and the ways they link with human activity.
- Dislike of violence, possibly a pacifist.
- Sometimes finds it difficult to relate to the material world.
- Feelings of having her 'head in the clouds', lack of groundedness.
- Inclined to be unrealistic.
- Sometimes overwhelmed by awareness, becoming unable to make decisions or to act.
- Shares some characteristics of the EMOTIONAL type.

Mental (Energy = Understanding)

- Likes to think things through.
- Strong belief in the power of the mind.
- Usually intellectual, enjoys using logical powers.
- Ability to be extremely rational, even in very difficult situations.
- Good use of reasoning power.
- Often articulate and precise.
- Enjoys reading.
- Interested in modern technology.
- Interested in scientific explanations, might question religious beliefs.
- Likes things to be 'proved to be true'.
- Inclined to find it difficult to comprehend SPIRITUAL and EMOTIONAL 'types'.

Emotional (Energy = Feeling)

- Aware of own feelings.
- Sometimes becomes overwhelmed by other people's feelings.
- Very sensitive in many ways, can laugh and cry easily.
- Highly creative but not always able to express this creativity.
- Experiences mood swings, from high to low and back.
- Great awareness of the pain of others.
- Working or looking for work in the caring professions.
- Interested in spiritual matters.
- Strongly intuitive.
- Sometimes finds it difficult to be organized, logical or rational.

Physical (Energy = Action)
- Essentially a 'doer'. Likes to be out in the world 'making things happen'.
- Strong, enduring energy.
- Enjoys sport or other outdoor pursuits.
- Sometimes appears to be aggressive.
- May need to be 'on the go' all the time.
- Adventurous, enjoys socializing, likes organizing.
- Sometimes afraid to take time to 'stand and stare'.
- At times will appear to be spiritually and/or emotionally insensitive.
- Shares some characteristics of MENTAL 'type'.

Count up your score for each section. Are you balanced throughout or do you have more ticks in one section than another? Do your ticks denote personal strengths or weaknesses? What do your answers tell you about your own energy?

Discover where you block your energy. Are you over-emotional or under-emotional? Are you lacking in spirituality? Do you give too much importance to your mental activity or are you unable to understand in a logical way? Are you only happy when you are actively 'doing' or are you afraid to go out into the world? Perhaps you are so spiritually and emotionally sensitive that you are unable to make rational decisions about how to act assertively. We are all different; our energy combinations are unique and they are always changing. However, it is useful to recognize where our energy is weak and where it is strong.

EXERCISE:

Using Your Spiritual, Mental, Emotional and Physical Energy

Think of a situation which was difficult for you, but you coped well and resolved the problem and maintained high self-esteem.

- How was your spiritual energy? Were you self-aware? Were you able to connect with the larger picture so that you were able to keep the difficulty in perspective?
- Did you have a clear understanding of what was going on? Were you able to be logical and rational when necessary? How would you describe your mental energy in this situation?
- Were you in touch with your feelings? Were you clear about your own and others' feelings? Was your emotional energy well balanced?
- How did you act? Did you clearly express your feelings and emotions in your physical actions? Were you able to be assertive?

Describe the situation and your energy levels by filling in Table 1.

Table 1

The situation was	The ways I would describe my energy levels			
	Spiritual	*Mental*	*Emotional*	*Physical*

Achieving Balance

When women come together and discuss their energy in this way, there is always a familiar theme. Inevitably most women find that their energies are most vibrant along the spiritual-emotional axis. If we look back to Figure 2 on page 5 we can see that our female energies are encompassed by our spirit and our emotions. Indeed, women have traditionally been seen as the embodiment of the spiritual and emotional energies – receptive, intuitive and waiting for the male of the species to act! The truth is that to be balanced and high in self-esteem we need to use both our male and female energies. If we only access our female energy, we will be unable to take our own power because we will have given it away to men. Take your male energies (your logic and rationality and your powers to act effectively and decisively) and combine them with the wisdom of your spirit and your emotions to create your own reality. So many women have lost the power of their inner male and are looking for this power in the wrong place. Take a look at Figure 10 on page 36. Consider the energies of the inner male and inner female. If your female energies are stronger than your male energies, you may be compensating by looking for these lost energies in a man. We attract to ourselves whatever we need, and if we need to become strong in our mental and physical capacities we may well attract to ourselves a relationship which seems to help us to create this balance in our lives.

Although the following example uses stereotypes, it does go some way to help explain the amazing ways that human energy will try to resolve this imbalance. Let us imagine a meeting between an over-emotional woman and a super-rational man (the woman only identifying with female energies and the man only identifying with male energies). Our heroine and hero meet and fall madly in love. She is in love with his logical reasoning powers (how wonderful to be so in control!). She *needs* some rational energy in her life because she is out of balance in this department. He is bowled over by her spiritual and emotional qualities (how amazing to be so aware and intuitive!). He *needs* this energy in his life because he is completely out of touch with his feelings and awareness. And so romance blossoms as they each find the other so utterly fascinating and different. For as long as these two continue to look to each other to balance themselves, this relationship is doomed. As soon as a crisis develops, both parties will revert to their extreme positions. She will deal with the problem at an emotional level and he will look to his intellect for all the answers. At this stage their fascination for each other's differences turns to frustration and annoyance. The thing that drew them to each other becomes the thing that pulls them apart. Can you relate to this process? Has this ever happened to you in your own relationships?

The key lies in taking personal responsibility for *all* of our energy. If we look outside ourselves for balance, we are looking in the wrong place. If our hero and heroine learn to appreciate their differences and start to cultivate their own missing parts, their relationship will flourish because both of them will be developing, growing and becoming whole. She needs to develop her inner male and he needs to develop his inner female. Once we are actively working to balance our own energy, our relationships will improve. This is covered in more depth in Part 2.

Self-Appreciation

Your life is a precious gift. You are unique and amazing. You deserve the best. Do you believe these things?

Look in a mirror, look deep into your own eyes and say: 'I love you.' Could you do it? How did you feel when you were doing it?

The quality of the personal reality you create depends entirely upon your depth of self-appreciation. If you cannot love yourself, you will never feel that you are quite deserving of the best. What do you really think that you deserve?

When we use positive affirmations and creative visualization to re-pattern our lives, we are changing our old limiting and restrictive patterning in order to allow the good to come to us. I sometimes hear from people who say that although they are using these techniques, they have become stuck; the techniques aren't working; everything has slowed down. New positive patterns contradict our old ways of coping, so there may be a transition period before we let go of the old and take on the new. This period can be a testing time when nothing seems quite right. It is crucial that we trust our own process at this stage and know that we are allowing the good to come to us. As we are about to allow change to enter our lives, we might begin to question whether in fact we really deserve the best. This happens at a deep level because the biggest challenge we face is to be able to love ourselves at all times, even when we feel unlovable and totally worthless. The power of re-patterning techniques depends entirely upon this basic affirmation: 'I, [name], love and value myself.'

Whenever you feel stuck in the growth process, say this affirmation. Affirming this positive belief will allow you to receive what you have been asking for. Don't give up on your other affirmations and your supporting visualizations – they all work! We become immobilized when we don't believe that we deserve to get what we want: on those days we will find it very hard to love ourselves. Why should this be so difficult?

It is easy to feel self-love when we are seeing ourselves as kind, thoughtful, positive, energetic, caring... in fact, when we are demonstrating any of the attributes we admire. It is not so easy when we are having thoughts which are not quite so lovable and experiencing emotions that are not really 'acceptable' to us.

QUESTIONNAIRE:

How I Like to See Myself/Don't Like to See Myself

What patterns of behaviour, thought and feeling do you admire in yourself? What patterns do you think are less than admirable? Put a Y for 'yes' after the words which describe the ways that you like to see yourself. Put an N for 'no' after the words which describe the ways that you don't like to see yourself.

MEAN	THOUGHTFUL	MOODY
KIND	NEEDED	THIN
GENEROUS	JEALOUS	HAPPY
ANGRY	RESPECTABLE	CARING
CONTROLLED	FAT	UNKIND
BORING	EMOTIONAL	ENERGETIC
SELFISH	HUMOROUS	RESENTFUL
GIVING	BUBBLY	SAD
INTELLECTUAL	DEPRESSED	UNATTAINABLE
DULL	TIGHT	ABLE
ROMANTIC	SERENE	BLOATED
SNAPPY	ADDICTED	TEMPERAMENTAL
OUT OF CONTROL	PEACEFUL	OLD
SPIRITUAL	SEXUAL	VIOLENT
FRIENDLY	ATTRACTIVE	ARTICULATE
POPULAR	CULTURED	NARROW-MINDED
INCOMPETENT	CAPABLE	ACTIVE
GRACEFUL	STUPID	EMBARRASSED
EDUCATED	CLUMSY	SOPHISTICATED
HAIRY	UP-FRONT	NON-JUDGEMENTAL
REFINED	MYSTERIOUS	BIGOTED
ATTRACTIVE	WEAK	LITERARY
FLABBY	SPARKLING	SEDUCTIVE
JOYFUL	SENSUAL	HUNGRY
NEEDY	WITHDRAWN	USEFUL
HEALTHY	CREATIVE	CONFIDENT
AGGRESSIVE	RELIABLE	GREEDY
IDIOTIC	ASSERTIVE	NEGATIVE
SUCCESSFUL	SOOTHING	COMPETITIVE

We have all been some of these things at some time. We are each capable of feeling any human emotion; there is an infinite choice available. This list of human patterns creates a strong and unique emotional response in all of us.

EXERCISE:

How I Most Like to See Myself/How I Most Dislike Seeing Myself

1a Choose the four words from the above questionnaire with which you most like to identify – the words with the most powerful 'yes':

....

....

1b Think carefully about *why* these descriptions are meaningful to you. Are they linked with certain values?

....

....

1c Are they part of your image?

....

1d Is it important that other people see you like this? If so, why is it important?

....

1e How do you feel on the days when you are not displaying these characteristics?

....

When I first started exploring my spirituality, it was very important to me that I appeared calm and peaceful. I wanted people to see that I was a 'spiritual person'. There were many, many times when I didn't feel the least bit calm, because of course we *cannot* always be centred and serene. I had two very young children at the time and the way I *wanted* to be and the way I really felt were miles apart. I didn't like the part of me that was tired, irritable and stretched; my vision and my reality were different. I set myself up for a hard time because I didn't understand that it was all right to feel these conflicting emotions. In fact, my spiritual development would have been greatly enhanced if I could have let myself off this hook of saintly perfection. We need to recognize that we are creatures of many, many parts and that it is only by understanding this psychological truth that we can free ourselves. If we keep beating ourselves up (metaphorically speaking!), we will remain powerless victims with low self-esteem.

2 Have you ever beaten yourself up?

This covers a whole range of thoughts and behaviours. You may have negative thoughts about being 'stupid' or 'no good' or 'not good enough'. We have *all* experienced thoughts like these and they only bring us down. Perhaps you criticize yourself verbally. Do you ever tell people how useless, pathetic and no good you are? Some people actually do themselves physical harm: head-banging, face-slapping and other punishments. All of these thoughts and behaviours are common. If you do any or all of these things, you are not odd; you are one of the majority. This majority is low in self-esteem and is disempowered. So if you hate the secret part that criticizes and/or injures yourself, you can let yourself off the hook. The way to stop self-destructive behaviour is to be kind to ourselves and to *accept* the parts which we find so difficult to acknowledge.

3a Choose the four words from the questionnaire with which you least like to identify – the words with the most powerful 'no':

....

....

3b Why don't you like these characteristics?

....

3c Do you have value judgements about the type of people who demonstrate these features?

....

3d Where do these values come from?

....

3e How do you feel about yourself when you display these patterns?

....

You might be wondering whether I am advocating antisocial or dangerous behaviour. I am not saying, for example, that it's OK to be angry and to express that anger in ways that hurt others. All I am saying is that we need to be able to accept any angry feelings that we might have. If we deny our anger and hate ourselves for feeling angry, we are creating a volcano of unexpressed and violent emotion which will eventually erupt.

Some emotions and actions are taboo. There is a cultural imperative not to display anger, especially if you are a woman! It is considered 'not nice' for women to be jealous or resentful or hairy or aggressive or fat. These are just a few examples of many cultural and family patterns which we learned as little girls. However, we also learned that it was fine to be caring, gentle, feminine, pretty, thin and respectable!

4 What did you learn about how women were meant to be?

....

5 Do these learned patterns of belief affect the ways you feel about yourself now?

....

6 What did you learn about how women are not meant to be?

....

7 Do these learned patterns affect your life now?

....

The truth is that our emotions will only cause us pain if we deny them. It is not necessary to act out every resentful and violent thought. It is only necessary to accept that we are having these thoughts and that they will pass and change. When we deny anything in our lives, we give that thing power over us. Whatever it is, it will keep emerging in some way until we finally accept it. We will look at the practical consequences of denying thoughts, behaviours and emotions in Part 2.

Self-appreciation is the key that opens the door which allows good to come to us. By using positive affirmations and creative visualization we can create new, powerful realities for ourselves. Self-appreciation requires that we love and value all parts of ourselves. This can be tricky, particularly when we are in the middle of a pattern that we find hard to love. Last week I found myself in the depths of one of my least favourite emotions – resentment. I like to see myself as a person who has everything under control; I like to be in charge and I don't mind hard work! However, last week I felt tired and all of my commitments were just a burden to me. I began to feel resentment towards my nearest and dearest family and this swiftly grew to embrace anybody whom I met who appeared to be relaxed and enjoying themselves. My resentment knew no bounds and became all the more terrible as I began to feel guilty… and so it went on and on. I began to write this piece, and as I wrote about the need to appreciate all parts of ourselves, I realized what I had been doing. I told myself that it was OK to feel resentment, even though I had created my own workload. I then gave myself some time off and had extra sleep. I repeatedly said, 'I love and value myself' – even though it was very hard to say at first. I stopped feeling guilty and I even forgave myself for shouting at my husband. Even when you know the theory, even if you write the books about it, you will still need to remind yourself that *you are always a lovable and valuable person.*

Part 2
A New Woman

4

Women in Love

Unconditional love means keeping your heart open all the time. To do so, you may need to let go of the expectations you have of other people, of wanting them to be anything other than what they are. It means letting go of any need for people to give you things, act in certain ways, or respond with love.

(SANAYA ROMAN, *PERSONAL POWER THROUGH AWARENESS*)

Our intimate love relationships do not run on unconditional love – not unless we have reached saintly status. (By intimate love relationships, I am referring to close sexual relationships.) We might well be working towards letting go of our expectations of others, but this is always an ongoing process. Let us be quite clear about this. Our life is a process of development and the nature of our relationships reflects our development exactly. While we are creatures of this material world our intimate love relationships will be based on conditional love. Some people tell me that they would never become involved in a relationship which was bound by anything less than unconditional love. Although many of us are working towards developing our potential to love without any restrictions and limitations, I have yet to see an intimate love relationship which is not bound by *any* conditions. We are creatures of need; if we can accept this, then we can let ourselves off the hook of spiritual perfection. This hook is one which women in particular prefer!

'Needs must' so the saying goes, and our needs must be met if we are to feel loved, valued and respected by our partner.

(I refer to heterosexual relationships here, although the same energetic processes will be found in gay relationships.) So let's stop pretending that we are only spiritual in nature; it is dangerous to think like this. Remember that our self-esteem depends upon the balance of our female *and* male energy.

We bring all our patterns to the arena of intimacy, both the positive and the negative. We cannot fail to bring everything: the good, the bad, the beautiful and the ugly. When we are involved in close love relationships, we cannot hide negative patterns because eventually even our closely guarded secrets become obviously 'closed' areas which require a lot of energy to keep hidden. In the end we have a number of choices:

- to 'come out' and admit our problem;
- to give up on developing the relationship but to stay in it;
- to leave the relationship so that we don't have to admit the problem;
- to 'come out' and then find that it is time to leave the relationship.

Well, how does all this theoretical chat help you? When the going gets rough and the loving feelings change, it is very important to regain your personal power and self-esteem. First you take Step 1 of the Five-Step Programme for Change (see page 44). You assess the situation and you make this assessment by using the strong theoretical basis which we have established. Remember that our thought, feeling and behaviour patterns have been learned through cultural and family conditioning. We bring all our patterns to our relationships. We tend to recreate the scenarios of our childhood, even if we were hurt. We can be obsessed by repeating our old hurts because:

- they are what we recognize and so at a very deep level we feel secure (the devil we know);
- if we keep repeating the pattern, there is always a chance that we might break it.

We looked earlier at the case of Mary whose father left when she was very small (page 20). You may remember that Mary's relationships with men were characterized by the repeating patterns of her relationship with her father. She had needy and clinging affairs with men who were emotionally distant. This reflected exactly what had happened with her father. She needed her father and feared her abandonment by him, but she also had to 'prove' that he had been 'right' to leave her. At some very deep level, Mary believed that her father must have been 'right' to go. If he was 'right' (as parents must be to the tiny child), then she must have been 'wrong' in some way. It must have been her fault that he left, so she did not deserve a good stable relationship with a man. After countless, disastrous intimate relationships, Mary began to recognize the interweaving threads of repeating patterns. Each bad relationship provided her with yet another chance to stop her father going (by stopping her man leaving) and of course she had set it up so that this was always impossible. Mary's behaviour within her intimate relationships appears to have been wholly emotional and irrational. How could she ever believe that she could stop her father leaving when he had been long gone? How could she want to repeat her terrible feelings of neediness and abandonment? Why did she put herself through so much pain for so long?

The truth is that when we are deep in our patterning we *are* wholly emotional and irrational! (Men also act in this way.) Our patterning remains addictive for as long as it is unconscious. Until we recognize the patterns which govern us, we cannot be free, but remain like marionettes with our patterns pulling our strings. It is so much easier to see other people's patterns than it is to see our own. But awareness is a magic key which sets us free from all our illogical and victim-like knee jerk reaciions.

LOVE AND INTIMACY

For us marriage is a journey toward an unknown destination... the discovery that people must share not only what they don't know about each other, but what they don't know about themselves.

(MICHAEL VENTURA,
SHADOW DANCING IN THE MARRIAGE ZONE)

Our patterns are all the ways in which we think, feel and act. Because we bring our whole selves to every experience, we must by definition be bringing all of our patterns to our intimate love relationships. This is why our intimate exchanges cannot be based on unconditional love. While we operate in the dark (unconscious patterns) in any area of our lives, we cannot offer unconditional love. The point is to stop trying to create 'perfect' relationships and to discover exactly what personal expectations and conditions we bring with our love.

Figures 14a and 14b demonstrate the ways that we can develop our awareness within a relationship. The circles are a diagrammatic representation of a relationship with my partner (called 'you'). In Figure 14a, there is a large shadowy area encompassing all that I don't know about you and all that I don't know about myself. In Figure 14b I have an increased awareness of our relationship. I know more about me because I am looking at my

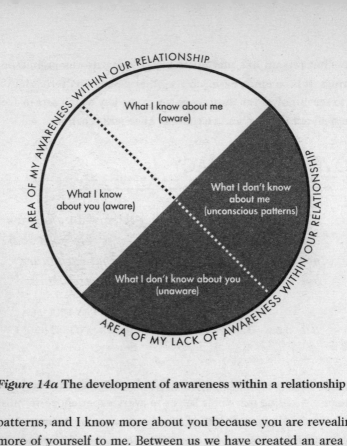

Figure 14a The development of awareness within a relationship

patterns, and I know more about you because you are revealing more of yourself to me. Between us we have created an area of intimacy, disclosure, sharing, confidentiality and trust. This enables us both to learn more about ourselves and about each other. Our feelings of personal self-worth and mutual self-respect will be enhanced and we will both feel increased self-esteem.

All of our relationships are based on exchanges of energy (our energies include all of our patterns, conscious and unconscious). This may seem an unromantic way to talk about love, but it offers a very real and practical approach to understanding our love lives. Light romantic fiction will keep us in an impossible dream world. Maybe that is what true romance is all about for some people – it is elusive, idealized, fictional and non-threatening. True intimacy is about closeness, confidentiality and trust and

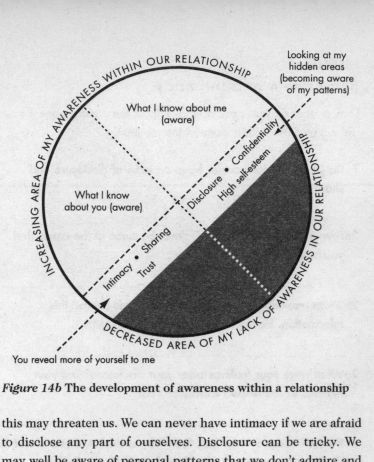

Figure 14b The development of awareness within a relationship

this may threaten us. We can never have intimacy if we are afraid to disclose any part of ourselves. Disclosure can be tricky. We may well be aware of personal patterns that we don't admire and would rather not share. There will be areas of vulnerability which we have hidden from ourselves (for 'protection') and we won't want to look in these dark and hidden places. If we bring these patterns to light, we may not want to share these 'secrets' in case we are not loved any more. True intimacy might feel risky, but the real risk lies in lack of intimacy.

While we believe that we need to keep things hidden, we live in fear and have little self-respect. We are continually afraid that we will be 'found out' and we feel low in self-esteem while we hide 'unworthy' parts of ourselves from our loved ones.

EXERCISE:

Self-Esteem and Intimacy

Look at your present close relationship or the previous one if you are not involved with anyone at the moment.

1 Do you and your partner have an area of disclosure and sharing?   Yes/No

2a If your answer to 1 is 'yes', describe some of the issues that *you* have disclosed:

....

2b Try to remember your feelings *before* you shared this information. How was your self-esteem? I felt:

....

2c What were your feelings *after* your disclosure? Did your feelings of self-respect increase? I felt:

....

3 If your answer to 1 is 'no', then why is this? Are you afraid to share? Is your partner afraid to share? We don't have a confidential, sharing area in our relationship because:

....

Trust, disclosure, intimacy and high self-esteem are all part of a relationship which is growing and developing in a healthy way. If your intimate relationship is nurturing, then both partners will be involved in a process of change and growing awareness. They will support each other emotionally and the relationship will be based on mutual respect and self-esteem.

If you have no commitment to sharing, or if this area is underdeveloped, then something is wrong. This is not a nurturing relationship and it does not value you. You will have low self-esteem for as long as your close relationship continues to devalue you. We will look at the possible reasons for your involvement in such a relationship throughout the rest of this chapter.

The basic beliefs which we learned as baby girls will control our adult lives unless we become conscious of them and begin to change them. The things we learned about love and intimacy when we were babies may be stopping us from having a truly ~ nurturing relationship in our adulthood. What have you learned about love and intimacy? Work through the following questionnaire to see how your beliefs affect your love life.

QUESTIONNAIRE:
What Do You Believe About Love and Intimacy?

	True	Untrue

- It's hard to trust men.
- Men often intimidate me.
- I am frightened by intimacy.
- I don't trust myself.
- I am addicted to behaviours which make it impossible for me to have an intimate relationship.
- I am always looking for love.
- True love is always painful.
- I deserve love.
- I am unlucky in love.
- If I love someone, they will abandon me.
- I cannot be intimate because I will lose my freedom.
- Long-term relationships are boring.

- I don't know how to show love.
- I'm always afraid to get close in case I am
  rejected.
- I like to keep myself to myself.
- I find it hard to be committed to one person.
- I love myself.
- Love belongs to fairy tales.
- There can be no good sex without love.
- Love is everywhere.
- Love is always disappointing.
- I can never show the real me.
- No one will ever really love me.
- I expect too much from a love relationship.
- I need someone who will take care of me.
- Falling in love is too much hassle.
- My love life is a disaster.
- I don't need love.
- I can see a recurring theme in my intimate
  relationships.
- I just want someone who needs me.
- Sex is frightening.
- I am too old to fall in love.
- When affairs become relationships, the sex is
  ruined.
- I am jealous of my partner's friendships.
- I deserve to enjoy sex.
- I am abused in intimate relationships.
- I am ready to change the patterns which
  deny me love and intimacy.

Consider your answers to this questionnaire. What did you learn about love when you were a child? How do these beliefs affect your intimate love relationships? Look at any negative beliefs which you know do affect your love life.

Think about the ways that your parents demonstrated their intimate feelings. Were your parents able to express their love for you? Were your parents able to express their love for each other? Has their behaviour affected your ability to be loving and intimate?

EXERCISE:
Changing Your Negative Beliefs About Love and Intimacy

Take one of your negative beliefs from the questionnaire, eg, 'If I love someone they will abandon me.' Rewrite a positive affirmation to replace the old belief, eg, 'I am secure in love.'

1 My negative belief is:

....

2 My positive affirmation is:

....

Positive Affirmations for Love and Intimacy

Remember that beliefs are only thoughts that we have learned and that we think are true. We can change these thoughts if they are not working for us. Some of the beliefs in the questionnaire are very positive affirmations. If these are true beliefs for you, then love and intimacy will not be problematic. However, most of us abound in non-trusting, non-deserving and fearful beliefs about love which we learned by watching and sensing our parents' relationships with each other and with us.

Create your own affirmations which contradict any negative

beliefs about love and intimacy. Say them, sing them, write them, repeat them again and again until you have replaced your old negative thoughts. The following affirmations will help you to create positive energy in the area of love and intimacy. When you can believe that you truly deserve love and support, then you will attract a nurturing, loving and intimate relationship which supports your self-esteem.

- I deserve love.
- I am lucky in love.
- I love myself.
- Love is everywhere.
- I deserve to enjoy sex.
- Love surrounds me.
- The more we share, the closer we get.
- I am lovable.
- It is safe for me to love.
- I attract love.

You can increase the power of affirmations by looking into a mirror and saying them out loud while looking deeply into your own eyes. Affirmations work – they are incredibly powerful! If you feel silly saying things that you don't believe just keep going. If you feel that nothing is happening, just keep going. If you feel a massive resistance, keep going – positive affirmations work by unearthing negativity. Remember that we are what we believe we are and that negative beliefs can be changed. If your beliefs about love and intimacy are not creating nurturing and validating relationships for you, then why don't you change them?

You are a unique and lovable person who deserves a loving intimate relationship which supports your self-esteem.

Repeating Patterns and Intimate Relationships

> *If, as a child, you looked for love and found pain,
> then as an adult you will find pain instead of love
> until you release your old family pattern.*

(LOUISE HAY,
LOVE YOURSELF, HEAL YOUR LIFE WORKBOOK)

Whatever emotions and behaviours were displayed in your childhood home, they will be the same ones that you look for in your adult relationships.

1 Why did your last relationship end?

....

2 Why did the one before that end?

....

3 Why did the one before that one end?

....

4 Is there a pattern? If so what is it?

....

Repeating Patterns – A Case Study

Perhaps you just always seem to choose the wrong sort of man. Frances comes from a family where her father frequently hit her and her brother and mother. She grew to accept this behaviour, but although it felt 'normal' within her family, she never told anyone about the beatings. Her father died when she was 18 and almost immediately Frances found herself in a relationship with a woman-hater. She did everything she could to make him pleased with her, but in the end nothing worked. Frances has had two short-term and two long-term relationships with men who hit her. She says now that something in her wanted to be abused.

'I hated seeing my mother being beaten up. She tried so hard to please my dad and I felt sorry for her. She never stood up to him, even when he beat us kids. I thought this must be what other people did at home, although a bit of me was ashamed of it so I kept quiet. When dad died, I was relieved for mum's sake, but she just went to pieces and started to drink heavily. She talked about him as if he had been a saint. When I thought about the way he had hurt us all, I felt guilty as if I was betraying the family. I don't know what my brother thinks because we have never discussed it. I soon met a young chap who was a bit mixed up and I felt sorry for him. I helped him out a bit and then we moved in together. He was really confused and he hated women, so I tried to show him how nice I could be. I kept waiting for him to be all right, but nothing changed much and then he started hitting me. Looking back now, I can see that as soon as he became physically violent, I became completely hooked on him. He left me and I met someone who was kind and thoughtful. This man was so nice to me, I just couldn't stand it. I felt totally bored by the relationship and I thought that he was a fool to be treating me so well. How could he care for me when I was such a worthless person? He kept trying to build me up and give me confidence, but I thought he was just an idiot, so I left and went looking for a man who had no illusions about me. It was easy to find another woman-hater; there are plenty around.

'I can see now that I set myself up to repeat the sort of relationship my mother had with my dad. There are lots of 'needy' men around and I still fancy them like mad, but I know that they are bad for me. I am trying to break this pattern and I have met other women who have had similar experiences. It's funny that when I hear another woman say that she has been beaten by a man, I feel so mad and yet I used to think that it was OK for someone to knock me around. It's easier to recognize a pattern in another woman's behaviour than it is to see it for yourself. My self-esteem was so low that I thought I deserved all that I was getting. I am seeing a counsellor and I belong to a women's group because I need all the support I can get to change. There is still a part of me that is drawn like a magnet to men who hate women; it is so powerful, it's almost like an addiction.'

When we are deep within our patterns, we are indeed addicted. We have an obsessive need to repeat these patterns over and over again so that we can right the original wrong (which is, of course, impossible) and because the ritual of the pattern is so comfortable (even if we are beaten black and blue). If Frances kept being physically abused, then her dad must have been right and she must have been wrong. We so want our parents to have been right, and if that means we were wrong then surely we deserve to be hit! This is confused logic certainly, but it is as powerful as any drug.

Exchanging Energy and Making Deals

Energetically speaking, we are always making deals. Our thoughts, feelings and actions are forms of energy which we bring to all our relationships. We are constantly involved in relationships with other people's energy patterns. At a very practical level, we can see our relationships in the form of energy transfer and exchange. What energy are we prepared to input for what return? What conditions and expectations do we bring to our relationships? Every energetic deal has a cost and a return.

EXERCISE:

The Price You Pay for the Deal You Make

Think about your present love relationship. (If you are not involved with anyone at the moment, look back at your last relationship.) What expectations and conditions are involved in this relationship? What are you prepared to do in order to get what in return? Think carefully about this; there is a lot involved. The answers to these two questions constitute the deal and the price that you are making with your partner.

If you are involved in a relationship at the moment, the following questions may be very difficult to answer, so please don't worry if you can't write anything. It is easier to complete this exercise if you are thinking of a past relationship which is over. If the deal is off, then the price got too high for someone. The terms of the deal are then more obvious, so we can have some perspective on the situation.

1 The deal is that:

....

2 Do you pay a price for this deal? If so, what do you think is the price?

....

3 How does this price affect your levels of self-esteem?

....

Let's look at Frances's relationships again. She left her husband Ben (the last man who physically abused her) when he started to hit their baby girl. Up to that time the deal had been that Frances took care of Ben and was his emotional support when he was down. In return he gave her the chance to be needed and allowed her to feel like a martyr with low self-esteem. They supported each other's compulsive patterns – hers to be the victim and his to be the abuser. This deal worked until Ben hit their baby, and even then Frances did not realize what had really been happening in their relationship. It was very difficult to leave Ben (she didn't want to abandon him; who would take care of him?). Frances only left because she wanted to protect her baby. It was months later when she realized the nature of the destructive patterns involved. Our patterns pull our strings until we become aware of them. The price that Frances was paying for the deal she made with Ben just got too high. Emotionally she could not afford to see her baby suffer, and this broke her pattern of being addicted to abusive relationships. She removed her baby from a violent home and told other people what was going on. She broke the patterns of thoughts, emotions and actions which had kept her mother trapped and unable to remove her own daughter (Frances) from a violent father. Frances felt the return of her self-respect when she took action to change the pattern. She changed her circumstances by:

- assessing her situation;
- deciding what she would like to change;
- specifying her preferred outcome;
- recognizing the negative patterning involved;
- changing her negative patterns.

These are the steps of the Five-Step Programme for Change introduced in Chapter 3. It is interesting to note that awareness of patterns is not the motivator for change. We do not recognize our patterns until we feel uncomfortable enough to need to change. It is this discomfort that promotes our awareness of our compulsive patterns and motivates us to change.

When being in love means being in pain
we are loving too much.

(ROBIN NORWOOD, *WOMEN WHO LOVE TOO MUCH*)

EXERCISE:
Your Love Relationships

These may be very difficult questions to answer. If it all feels too much, just leave this exercise for another time.

1 Have your love relationships ever caused you emotional
   pain?   Yes/No

2 If 'yes', then can you describe the situations and the feelings?
   The situations were:

   ....

   ....

   The feelings were:

   ....

   ....

3 Did you let these situations repeat?   Yes/No

4 If 'yes', why did you let this happen?

   ....

   ....

5 Are you in a love relationship now which is causing you emotional pain?   Yes/No

6 Do you ever find yourself making excuses for your man?

Yes/No

7 If 'yes', when and how do you make these excuses? I make excuses for my man when:

....

....

I excuse him by saying and/or doing and/or thinking the following:

....

....

8 Why do you make excuses for him?

....

....

9 What are you trying to cover up?

....

....

10 Do you think that he needs your emotional support? If so, why does he?

....

....

11 Does your partner find it difficult to express his emotions?

Yes/No

12 Are you waiting for him to change?   Yes/No

DAMAGING RELATIONSHIPS

Why do so many women attract unsuitable and harmful intimate relationships where they play the victim with little or no self-esteem? And why do these women find it so difficult to leave their damaging relationships? Most of us, at some time or other, have made some poor bargains in the love department. The deals we made were based on poor decisions which had their foundations in our negative family and cultural thought, feeling and behaviour patterns.

Both women and men suffer emotional pain. Some women find this hard to believe because they have only ever had relationships with men who don't or can't show their pain. Cultural and biological factors affect the ways that women and men deal with their hurt. Many women are more inclined to internalize their childhood (and adult) pain and become obsessed with damaging relationships. Remember that women are inclined to over-identify with their inner female characteristics, developing and expressing their nurturing, sensitivity and emotions. Under stress we turn to the familiar 'ways of coping', and emotional caretaking is a pattern of behaviour that most of us women have learned.

Men are more inclined to externalize their childhood and adult pain, making it less personal by becoming obsessed with worldly pursuits such as work, sport and hobbies. Most men identify heavily with their inner male characteristics and in a difficult situation they will 'cope' in the ways that they learned in boyhood – in a rational and conceptual way (avoiding emotions at all costs).

Cultural patterning affects both women and men. If we have been encouraged to relate to our inner female (being taught that the action-planning, assertiveness, logical thinking and risk-taking is 'men's work'), then that leaves us with only the 'women's work' (nurturing, receptive and passive). If we run with this particular myth of 'what men are like', then we are left with a very ineffective role model for women. Look back to Figure 10, page 36. If you over-identify with female energy, then you will be involved with men who over-identify with their male energy. The energetic deal is clear. We are all (female and male) working towards wholeness. Energetically speaking, we are always trying to create a balance. If we do not work at balancing our own energy (so that we can be whole), then we will look outside ourselves for the parts that we need in order to feel balanced. If I am low on inner male energy, I will look for this energy elsewhere: I will be attracted to a man who is high in inner male energy (assertive, outgoing, conceptual, rational, logical). He will be attracted to me because I am out of balance. I have more than enough inner female energy (emotional, caring, sensitive, spiritual, receptive) and that is what he needs. So our traditional male (personifying inner male energy) and our traditional female (personifying inner female energy) are drawn to each other like moths to a flame.

Thus both women and men are attracted to damaging relationships which create a mutual lack of self-respect and self-esteem. An important difference between the sexes is demonstrated in the ways that men and women try to deal with such relationships:

- **Men cope by**: looking outside the relationship and becoming absorbed in activities.

- **Women say about this behaviour:** 'Doesn't he even realize that we have a problem here? The more I need his emotional support, the more distant he becomes.'

- **Women cope by**: looking at the relationship; trying to work out what is going on; looking at self; asking 'What have I done wrong?'; thinking 'What can I do to change this situation?'; trying to please the man; waiting for him to change.

- **Women say:** 'He really loves me; he's got so much potential, all he needs is my love, attention and help; I know just what he needs and if I can give him that then everything will be all right; I know he doesn't mean to be thoughtless; I don't take any notice when he's like that, he's basically got a heart of gold; if only I can be patient enough to wait; I know that it will all come right in the end.'

Yes, women and men both suffer emotional pain, but they try to deal with it very differently.

EXERCISE:
What Do You See in Your Man? – A Visualization

Read through these instructions and then find a quiet place where you will be able to do the exercise undisturbed. Have you a man in your life at the moment? This could be someone you are living with, having an affair with, sharing children with or just someone whom you think about a lot. (If you think about him frequently then he is still in your life!) If no one comes to mind, choose a person from a previous relationship.

Preparation for visualization

Now sit comfortably and relax your body. Close your eyes and take some deep breaths and follow your breathing in and out. Concentrate on the point between your breaths. When your mind wanders off, keep returning to this point. Your thoughts will continue; just observe them and return to your breath awareness. As your body becomes more and more relaxed and your thoughts drift far away, visualize an empty screen in your mind. If you cannot actually see a screen, don't worry; just know that it is there. For some people, visualization is a knowingness or awareness rather than an actual picture.

Visualization

When you are ready, visualize your man on the screen. If you can see him or be aware of him without the screen, then that's fine. See him in glorious technicolour. Observe him and become aware of the thoughts that you connect with him (for example: he's getting fat; he's just like his father; he's absolutely gorgeous; he's got no sense of style; why doesn't he get himself together? why is he always telling me what to do? he is such a kind man; he treats me well; how can I ever trust him? he just never shows his feelings; why doesn't he spend more time with the children? is he having an affair? he is a wonderful partner).

Your internal dialogue indicates the underpinnings of your relationship with this man. It demonstrates the conditions and expectations that you bring with your love. When you have done the visualization, write down the thoughts which accompanied your pictures.

1 Your thoughts about your man:

....

....

Go back through these thoughts one at a time and notice the feelings which surround them. Be aware of any bodily changes which occur during this process. Do your thoughts make you feel good or bad? Does your pulse quicken; your stomach knot; your body tense or relax? Do you feel exhilarated; comfortable and peaceful; anxious and nervous? Are your hands sweating; are you blushing; are you feeling dizzy; is your mouth dry; are you feeling wonderful? Make a note of your reactions.

2 Your feelings and bodily reactions to these thoughts:

....

....

Close your eyes again and ask yourself this question.

3 Does he remind me of anybody?

....

If he does, think about how you feel about this other person. If there is a powerful resemblance, you may even be getting your people confused. I remember a man shouting at me, 'I am not your father!' I was shocked and retaliated with anger, but he was right; I was relating to a memory rather than to a real person.

Close your eyes again and imagine telling your man about this exercise. Could you do it? Are there some things you couldn't say? If so, what are they and why can't you share them with him?

4 Thoughts and feelings that I can't share:

....

....

5. My reasons for not sharing this information:

....

....

Cycles of Damage

When we were discussing love and intimacy, we saw that the ways to develop our intimate relationships depended upon disclosure, sharing and trust. Figure 14b on page 83 shows how couples can become closer by looking at hidden areas and then sharing that information with each other. If you are learning about yourself, then it is important to be able to communicate this understanding in order to develop a caring and trusting relationship. If you are unable to express your feelings and needs within your relationship, then it cannot be intimate or close. If our emotional needs are not being met within our close relationships, then we are participating in damaging relationships. Damaging relationships create troubled families where communication is unclear and both parents and children feel unaccepted, invalidated and low in self-esteem. Children of troubled families repeat their learned negative patterning and grow up looking for damaging relationships. Figure 15 shows how this happens.

Women in damaging relationships make poor deals based on negative patterns which they have learned from their culture and from their families. If you are having difficulty in recognizing your negative patterning, look to all your thoughts and beliefs about your womanhood that start like this: I/women *should;* I/women *must,* I/women *have to.*

Do you fear intimacy? If you do, it is because you are afraid to trust. Lack of trust is rooted in old childhood memories. In her marvellous book, *Women Who Love Too Much,* Robin Norwood describes a fine example of how mistrust is developed in the young child.

The parents of the child are fighting and arguing and the child feels afraid. The child asks her mother why she is angry with her daddy. Mother, looking angry and upset, denies that anything is wrong. Mother gets cross with the child and says that she will be angry if the child keeps on. The child now feels fear, confusion,

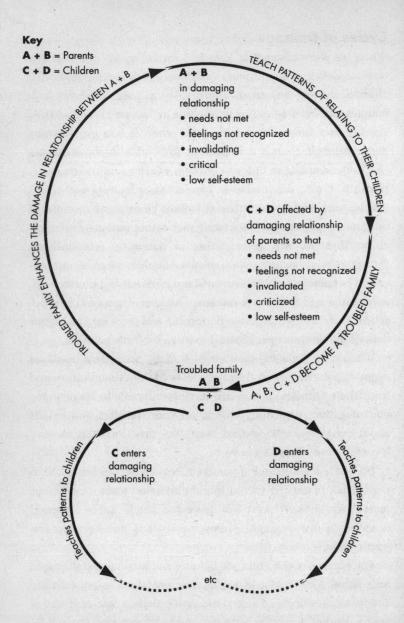

Key
A + B = Parents
C + D = Children

TEACH PATTERNS OF RELATING TO THEIR CHILDREN

A + B
in damaging
relationship
• needs not met
• feelings not recognized
• invalidating
• critical
• low self-esteem

C + D affected by
damaging relationship
of parents so that
• needs not met
• feelings not recognized
• invalidated
• criticized
• low self-esteem

TROUBLED FAMILY ENHANCES THE DAMAGE IN RELATIONSHIP BETWEEN A + B

A, B, C + D BECOME A TROUBLED FAMILY

Troubled family
A B
+
C D

C enters
damaging
relationship

D enters
damaging
relationship

Teaches patterns to children

Teaches patterns to children

etc

Figure 15 Cycles of damage

anger and guilt. Mother has told her that she (the child) has got it wrong, but if she has, why does she (the child) feel so afraid? Now the child must make a choice between the devil and the deep blue sea. If the child is right, then her mother has lied to her and so she cannot trust her mother. Or, if the mother is right, then the child's perceptions are wrong and so she cannot trust her own judgements.

The young child is in a no-win situation and will usually make a confused compromise; after all, she cannot let her mother be wrong. And so she will allow her awareness and perceptions to become muddled and hazy so that she will not have to experience the pain of having her feelings invalidated. This early damage will affect the child's ability to trust herself, both in her own relationships with her parents and in her later adult relationships. She will certainly have a self-esteem problem.

If the parental relationship is fraught with difficulties, then there may be little time, inclination or energy left for the children to receive the love, affection and nurturing that they need. This need for love leaves a child with an empty, yearning place inside. She is aching for love, but she doesn't trust her own judgement and she feels that she doesn't deserve love. What a legacy of beliefs and feelings to take into her adult relationships!

A TENDER TRAP

To some degree this child is you! To some extent we are all from troubled families. However nurturing our background, we will all be struggling with issues of trust, deservability, self-worth and self-esteem. The process of becoming whole is about learning to love and accept all parts of ourselves, and so everyone (our parents, ourselves and our children) is working on these important issues. The extent of the damage will always be a question of degree. If the very tiny girl experiences only invalidation and criticism, then this abuse will have a profound effect on her close and intimate relationships. Because she has not received sufficient nurturing, she will try to fill this need by becoming a care-giver. By giving care and love, she can get close to a nurturing experience. When we link this idea of a need to be caring for someone in order to feel love (albeit vicariously) with the cultural expectations of womanhood (nurturing, sensitive, receptive etc), the implications become obvious. It is easy for us to walk into a tender trap of our very own making.

> *We are drawn to those who are needy, compassionately identifying with their pain and seeking to relieve it in order to ameliorate our own.*
>
> (ROBIN NORWOOD, *WOMEN WHO LOVE TOO MUCH*)

Think again in terms of male and female energy. If I need to be needed, then I will be looking for a needy man (and he will be looking for me!). During a recent workshop of 30 women, I asked how many had had a relationship with a 'needy' man; everyone put up their hands. We are drawn to those men whom we see as being most needy, and the exact type of neediness which attracts us depends precisely on our own patterns.

EXERCISE:
Your Favourite 'Needy' Type of Man

The following descriptions are of types of men. Choose the ones which most attract you.
- Can't seem to settle
- Wild and irresponsible

- Addicted to something
- Ill
- Poor
- Depressed
- Stubborn
- Unable to communicate with others
- Unable to communicate with you
- Distant and remote
- Intellectual and preoccupied
- Abuses you
- Macho type
- Unable to commit himself
- Unhappy
- Sexually confused
- Needs your total attention
- Cold and unemotional
- Just needs *you*
- Has financial problems
- Is a workaholic
- Angry and temperamental
- Creative and depressed
- Confused 'new man'
- Unreliable
- Mean and moody

Perhaps you feel that you are not attracted to any of these characteristics. Our patterning and the patterns we attract can be very subtle. What 'type' of man do you fancy like mad, even if you know that he will be bad for you?

When we appreciate ourselves and feel high in self-esteem, we only become involved in nurturing relationships. We do not need to be needed, and so we will not attract a 'needy' man who needs rescuing. Our learned patterns of thought feeling and behaviour are very deep, and although we may be working to balance ourselves and to take control of our lives, we always need to be on the look-out for our own self-invalidating patterns. If you are being drawn yet again into a caring role with a needy man, BEWARE!

EXERCISE:

Applying the Five-Step Programme for Change

If your intimate relationships are unsatisfactory and do not support you, then maybe it is time to change. Use the Five-Step Programme for Change to help you extricate yourself from damaging relationships in order to create a nurturing and balanced intimate relationship which is based on mutual respect and self-esteem.

1 Assess the situation

Try to be objective, although this might be hard. Look at your relationship with an observer's eye. Try to remain unemotional and really evaluate what is going on. If your best friend was having a relationship just like yours, what would you say to her?

....

....

2 Decide what you would like to change

What is it exactly that you don't like? Be specific and be honest.

Forget about being 'nice' and 'accepting', and allow your own needs to express themselves.

....

....

3 Specify your preferred outcome

Be very focused here. What is it that you really want in your relationship? Write down the positive outcomes that you want to create. Be clear, positive and assertive in your statements.

....

....

4 Recognize the negative patterning involved

This may be hard. There are many questions to ask here. Look at your self-beliefs; what do you think that you deserve? Look at your energy; is it balanced? Can you be assertive, directive, outgoing, logical and rational if you need to be? What are your deep beliefs about mens' and women's roles? Can you express your true feelings? Do you need to be needed?

....

....

5 Change the negative patterns – re-pattern your life

Use the techniques for change: affirmations, creative visualization, forgiveness, balancing your male and female energy and self-appreciation.

As you work on your own negative patterning, your life will change. When you feel that you deserve to be treated well, you will stop being a victim with no self-esteem. You will be free to walk away from any victim-type relationships in which you are involved. Abusers will no longer be drawn to you as you will have no 'victim energy' to attract them. You will be free to have supporting and loving intimate relationships with men who are working on their own patterning. You will attract men who will treat you well. Men who want relationships which are equal and nurturing will be drawn to your energy patterns.

Forgiveness and Letting Go

As we work to understand why we are what we are, we will unearth more and more negative patterning. Inevitably this will lead us on a trail of clues which will take us right back to our childhood. This journey will be full of insights which may be as painful as they are illuminating. Every time we recognize a negative self-belief, we can trace its source back to those who took care of us when we were very small. We may wonder *why* our mother, father, grandmother, grandfather, brother, sister, teacher, etc did not always validate and support our positive self-beliefs.

Why did my mother treat me like that? Why didn't my father show me that he loved me? Why did he hit me? Why did she let him abuse me? They always said that I was stupid at school and look how it ruined my life. If only she had left him, then it would have been all right for me. If only she hadn't left him, then it would have been all right for me...

When we begin to recognize the sources of our limiting beliefs, we feel angry. This is quite natural. Anger and disempowerment go hand-in-hand, and so every time we allow ourselves to be victimized, we store away our anger about it. As we begin to work on our negative patterning, we start to release this stored anger. (We will look more closely at the relationship between anger, disempowerment and empowerment in the following chapter.)

Forgiveness is a process of letting go. When we forgive someone, we are *never* condoning their behaviour. We are not saying that whatever they did to us was acceptable. We are saying that whatever they did was certainly *not* right; the process of forgiveness starts here, in the recognition of the wrongdoing. We cannot let go of anything until we are prepared to recognize it. Once we have done this, we release the many painful emotions which are part of the victim package – shame, anger, resentment, low self-esteem, guilt, fear, and so on. Before we can let go of these emotions, we need to allow ourselves to feel them. So let yourself feel them. They are only your emotions; they may feel intense, but this will pass. Your emotions will only hurt if you continue to deny them.

Now think about your own limiting thought, feeling and behaviour patterns. Have you discovered where they may have originated? Work through the following exercise, and as you do so, remember that you are beginning to let go of many emotions which support your victim status. You are a woman with self-esteem and you can forgive and let go of anything which holds you back from achieving your own true potential.

EXERCISE:
Last Day on Earth Forgiveness

1 I was invalidated as a child in the following way:

....

....

2 These limitations have affected my adult relationships by:

....

....

3 The people who invalidated me were:

....

....

4 My feelings about these people are:

....

....

Now choose the person whom you find most difficult to forgive. Read the following instructions through and then do the visualization.

Find a quiet place, sit comfortably and relax. Close your eyes and become aware of your breathing. If your thoughts crowd your mind, just go back to concentrating on your breathing. When you are ready, bring to mind your chosen person. You can see this person in front of you and you know that it is their last day on earth. You will never see this person again. What would you like to say to them? If you feel like shouting, then do it. If you feel like crying, then do it. This is your big chance to clear up your relationship. This person also wants to resolve the situation. He/she is listening to all that you have to say. When you have finished, let the other person speak. What are they saying? When the communication between you is over, hear yourself forgiving this person. Hold the picture of them in your mind and say out loud, 'I forgive you.'

Open your eyes and congratulate yourself on a magnificent effort. Forgiveness is hard work because it takes us deep into our patterning where we have to deal with heavy emotional issues. We can only forgive bit by bit and so you may have to repeat this visualization many times over a period of time. (Just when you think you have finally forgiven, up it all pops again.) The most important thing to remember is that every tiny scrap of forgiveness moves mountains of emotional pain.

Use this visualization for anybody you need to forgive, dead or alive. The strong intention to forgive is really all you need; the rest will take care of itself. Your self-esteem will rise as you leave your victim status behind and work towards letting go of everything which is holding you back.

WOMEN IN LOVE – IN CONCLUSION

This may have felt like a hard chapter to read; it was certainly hard to write. The nature of our adult, intimate love relationships is very closely linked with our early childhood experiences and recognizing this link may be painful.

We have seen that negative patterning has an addictive quality which can easily stay with us from the cradle to the grave and that escaping from any addiction is a powerful and intense process. As soon as we become aware of the family and cultural conditioning which has so profoundly affected our lives, we can choose whether to blame or to change. Blame permits us to repeat our negative patterning and to remain low in self-esteem. Change allows us to take control of our lives, to increase our self-esteem and to recognize our negative patterns as keys to our personal growth and development.

The Chinese use the same symbol for crisis as they do for opportunity. This provides an interesting and empowering way to view our limitations. If you have recognized a recurring negative theme in your relationships with men, then this will have certainly produced crises for you in the past. If your present intimate relationship is in crisis, take heart! Recognize this present crisis as an opportunity for you to learn, develop and change.

Life always shows us what we need to learn. What is your life showing you at the moment? What do you need to change? You know now that you have the power to change the patterns which aren't working for you, so go ahead and do it. Our relationships are always offering us insights into our own development and the trick is to recognize exactly what they are showing us.

Circle of Love Visualization
Read the following instructions right through before you do the visualization.

Relax, close your eyes and become aware of your breathing. When you are ready, imagine yourself in the centre of a circle of people. You recognize each person in the circle as someone who is or has been very close to you. Let the circle include your parents and your lovers. Your circle may be large or small, but every person will be meaningful to you. Look at each person in turn and ask yourself, 'What gift did this person bring me?' Remember that gifts are not always gift-wrapped; they are often disguised. Let each person step forward one at a time and hand you their gift. It doesn't matter if you don't know what it is; just take whatever they hand you and smile and thank them. Go right round your circle collecting your gifts. This is your circle of love. Everyone in your circle of love is there for a very important reason; they have each come to teach you something of great significance about yourself. When all your gifts are at your feet, dissolve your circle and come out of the visualization.

This is a very powerful exercise. You may have recognized some, many or none of the gifts. Eventually you will recognize all of them. Some gifts are very discreet and will take a while to come into awareness. Be prepared for the results of this visualization to occur at any time.

The most wonderful gift that I ever received was from a man who totally victimized me. Years later, as I finally crawled out of my victim's trap, I had learned many techniques to create self-esteem, enough to fill a book. Without this man's gift, I would never have begun my writing career. I thank him for his gift which certainly did not come gift-wrapped, but which changed a life of terrible crisis into one of glorious opportunity.

Addictions and Empowerment

*.... men may not be the only thing
we're hooked on. In order to block our
deepest feelings from childhood, some of us
have also developed dependencies
on addictive substances.*

(ROBIN NORWOOD,
WOMEN WHO LOVE TOO MUCH)

An addiction appears to be life-enhancing, but is really soul-destroying. Addictive behaviour is rooted in self-hate, and an addicted person has very low self-esteem. Many women are involved in some form of addictive behaviour to compensate for the fact that we have lost touch with our own truth and that now it is too painful for us to recognize our own emotional needs.

Perhaps you are wondering if you have any addictions. We can be addicted to men who are 'needy'. We may attract abusive relationships; overeat; undereat; drink too much; take drugs (illegal or prescribed); indulge in compulsive sex; shoplift; overspend; overwork; smoke; gamble... if we are compulsively using any behaviour to hide from ourselves, then we are addicted.

Let's return to the cradle where all our stories begin. Women with addictions were little girls from troubled families. In the previous chapter we saw how a damaging relationship between two adults creates a troubled family. All families, however nurturing in intent, suffer from 'trouble' to some degree – we can never get it perfect. We need to make a clear distinction between the definitions of the nurturing family and the troubled family as we use the concepts here.

THE NURTURING FAMILY

If your family was nurturing, you will have enjoyed growing up. Your parents will have had a supportive relationship which was built on mutual respect. Communication will have been as open as possible and family members will not have been afraid to express their feelings. The underlying feeling between family members will have been one of trust – you could trust each other and so you could trust yourself.

A nurturing family validates and supports its members and the children know that they are intrinsically worthy and lovable, even when they are punished for their behaviour. The parents are flexible and are able to recognize when it is time to change the boundaries (yes, you are old enough now to stay out later). The discipline has meaning and this is explained to the children. Discipline is fair but remains consistent until the rules change. Family members are able to talk about what is going on within the family. Feelings are aired and no one is afraid. Members of a nurturing family feel good about themselves and can trust their own feelings and perceptions. They have a sense of the benevolence of the universe and they are high in self-esteem.

THE TROUBLED FAMILY

Two people in a damaging, intimate love relationship can create a troubled family. Look back at Figure 15 on page 102. A damaging relationship runs on the following principles.

- Needs are not recognized or met.
- Feelings are not expressed.
- Behaviour is invalidating and critical.
- Low self-esteem prevails.

These negative thought, behaviour and feeling patterns undermine the child of such a relationship: she learns that she cannot trust her own instincts and perception and that the world is a frightening place. Small wonder if she grows up looking for a way to numb her pain!

DAMAGING RELATIONSHIP → TROUBLED FAMILY → DAMAGING RELATIONSHIP → TROUBLED FAMILY

And so the patterns pass from one generation to the next with each invalidating relationship creating children with low self-esteem who eventually produce troubled families of their very own (Figure 15). The cycle ends when someone breaks their own negative patterning and chooses a supportive and balanced relationship and creates a nurturing family.

Figure 16 shows the patterns within the nurturing family and the range of possible patterns within a troubled family. Of course every family has its problems, but the foundations of the nurturing family are found in a good supportive relationship between the parents who teach positive patterning to their children. As the diagram shows, the range of possible negative patterns is extensive. The 'troubled family' can be one which is sexually and physically abusive or one which is heavily critical and invalidating (mentally abusive). The extent and degree of the negative patterning involved is incomparable. If you come from a troubled family, you will be suffering the consequences according to your own particular experiences. It is highly likely that you will be involved in addictive behaviour to compensate yourself, hide from yourself and punish yourself.

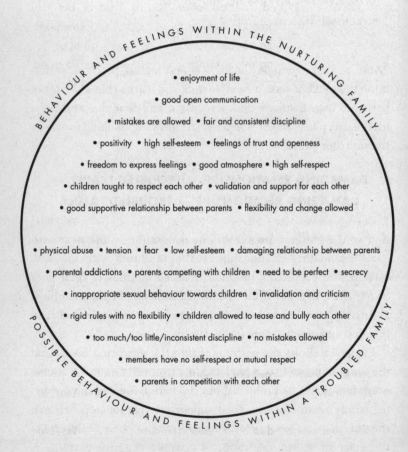

BEHAVIOUR AND FEELINGS WITHIN THE NURTURING FAMILY

- enjoyment of life
- good open communication
- mistakes are allowed • fair and consistent discipline
- positivity • high self-esteem • feelings of trust and openness
- freedom to express feelings • good atmosphere • high self-respect
- children taught to respect each other • validation and support for each other
- good supportive relationship between parents • flexibility and change allowed

- physical abuse • tension • fear • low self-esteem • damaging relationship between parents
- parental addictions • parents competing with children • need to be perfect • secrecy
- inappropriate sexual behaviour towards children • invalidation and criticism
- rigid rules with no flexibility • children allowed to tease and bully each other
- too much/too little/inconsistent discipline • no mistakes allowed
- members have no self-respect or mutual respect
- parents in competition with each other

POSSIBLE BEHAVIOUR AND FEELINGS WITHIN A TROUBLED FAMILY

Figure 16 **The nurturing family and the troubled family**

EXERCISE:
My Addictions

We can be addicted to chocolate, to abusive relationships with men or to not eating. There are so many ways we can be addicted to so many things. Some are life-threatening; others threaten our quality of life. We cannot compare our addictions. If you act compulsively in ways that punish yourself and numb your pain, you are addicted. Your addiction may be a secret, but please don't feel ashamed to answer these questions. Remember that most of us are from troubled families and nearly all of us have had or are having relationships with men who are no good for us (this is an addiction). Having several addictions is very common.

1 **My addictions are:**

....

....

2 **Are your addictions secret?**   Yes/No

3 **If your addictions are secret, why are they?**

....

4 **How do you feel about your addictions?**

....

....

5 **Can you imagine your life without your
   addictions?**   Yes/No

6 **Have you ever tried to break your addictions?**   Yes/No

7 **Would you like to break your addictive patterning?**   Yes/No

We become addicted because we are in pain. Our addiction numbs the pain and so we are afraid to release the addiction. You may need medical help or some other kind of professional help. You may need a counsellor and/or support group. When you are ready to change, you will not be afraid to ask for help. You will be amazed to find that many other people are acting out your 'secret' behaviours.

EXERCISE:

My Secret Behaviours Surrounding My Addictions

Make a list of all the behaviours surrounding your addictions which you have never told anybody about. Perhaps you ate your children's chocolate; kept a stash of alcohol in the car; stole money to pay for your addiction; lied to your loved ones to protect your secret; smoked cigarette butts from the pavement or rubbish bin; drank salt water to make yourself sick after an eating binge...

1 ....

2 ....

3 ....

4 ....

5 ....

6 ....

What is your most terrible secret? Did you write it down?

Now forgive yourself. Visualize yourself enacting your very

worst secret behaviour. Look at this picture of yourself in pain and say the following affirmation: 'I love you and I forgive you.'

You are addicted because you are full of self-hate. Your addiction numbs the pain and punishes you further so your self-hate is reinforced. Your recovery begins with self-forgiveness.

EXERCISE:
Living in My Family

Go back in time as far as you can until you are as young as you can remember. If this is hard, take a look at some photographs of yourself as a tiny girl toddling around. Can you remember your childhood home? Can you remember how it felt to be there with your parents? Close your eyes and try to recreate a scene from your babyhood. This tiny girl experienced joy and laughter, but she also experienced emotional pain. How could such a small person deal with her pain? Let's look at your family; how did they deal with life?

Answer the questions which are appropriate for you.

1 the type of relationship that your parents had with each other:

....

....

2 How would you describe the atmosphere in the house?

....

....

3 Were there any secrets in your house that you shared as a family? If so, what were they?

....

....

4 Did you have any secrets of your own as you grew up? If so, what were they?

....

....

5 I wish I had told my mother that:

....

....

6 I wish I had told my father that:

....

....

7 I wish that my parents had:

....

....

Forgive your parents – remember that they have parents too!

DISEMPOWERMENT, RAGE AND EMPOWERMENT

> *When you stop giving your power away to other people you won't feel angry any more.*
>
> (SHAKTI GAWAIN, *LIVING IN THE LIGHT*)

Addictive behaviour, low self-esteem, disempowerment and rage are intricately entwined. If we are addicted, then we are *angry*. We are really, really angry and we can trace our rage back to our babyhood. You may be addicted and unable to recognize your anger – perhaps that is what your addiction does for you, it keeps you from feeling your rage. Every time we were victimized in our childhood (whether our victimizer was conscious or unconscious of the fact), we stashed away our anger, deep down inside. Simultaneously we learned that we could not trust our own responses. Ambiguous parental messages confused the tiny girl and she was left unable to trust her instincts – leaving more anger hidden away. Every time we are disempowered, we are angry – we are talking about a volcano of unexpressed rage here!

In Chapter 2, we looked at moving out of blame and into empowerment by harnessing our personal power. Look at Figure 8 on page 26. There at the centre we are high in self-esteem and feeling empowered, we are focused on the present and are looking *inside* ourselves for direction and purpose. We are experiencing and creating our own personal power. If our self-esteem is threatened in some way, we have a tendency to take the pressure off by focusing on someone or something outside ourselves. We look outside, beyond our boundaries, and in so doing we let our personal power leak away.

When our addictions are in the spotlight we feel vulnerable. We would love to relieve the pressure by blaming something or someone, but of course this tactic does not work. As soon as we look outside ourselves for the answers, we become disempowered. When we make the important link between our addictive behaviour and the negative patterning of our early childhood, we start a powerful process. Because we have suppressed our power (and our anger) and numbed our pain for so long, the first sign of our empowerment is the return of angry feelings. (Our fear of our own anger can keep us in our addiction.) Our rage is inevitable, but fear is not. Before we can 'let go' of any thought, behaviour or feeling pattern, we need to face it and accept it. We can stay in denial over our anger for a lifetime, but if we do, we will always be disempowered, low in self-esteem and angry (denial *increases* our deep anger). Facing our true feelings is sometimes an intense experience, but our feelings only cause us pain when we deny them. If you have an addiction, then you will also have a volcano of rage which will start to bubble as soon as you understand the negative patterning underlying your condition. If you have no recognizable addiction but you are low in self-esteem, then you will also have plenty of hidden anger to bring to light.

If you have been feeling angry while working through this book, then this is a very positive sign that you are beginning to get in touch with your own personal power. Anger is only energy. As you move through the process of denial, acceptance and letting go, use this energy creatively. If you are afraid of causing harm in releasing your anger, then create a safe space where you can really let off steam, shout and thump pillows (or whatever you feel like doing). When you know that you are free to hit out in safety, you will not be afraid of this energy. When your anger becomes directed, you may need counselling support of some kind. At some stage you may need to stand your ground and express your anger in a meaningful way. It is OK to express your anger to another person, but do it in a non-blaming way. For example, rather than say 'You make me angry when you do that', try 'I feel angry when that happens'. There may be things to be said and you may need to say them, but find the right place, the right time and the right words to express and let go of your feelings.

As you work on accepting and letting go of your anger, your rage will diminish and you will become more assertive. As you reclaim your lost personal power, you will find that your self-esteem will rise and you will feel empowered to tackle the effects of negative patterning in your life. Your addictive behaviours (in relationships, with food, with drugs or whatever) can be changed.

You can only change by using your personal power. Your personal power lies within you. The past is over and the point of power is NOW!

EXERCISE:

Applying the Five-Step Programme for Change

Use the Five-Step Programme to help you to evaluate your situation.

1 Assess the situation

Describe your relationship with your addiction.

....

....

2 Decide what you would like to change

What don't you like about your condition? (Ignore negative thoughts about how it's too hard or impossible to change.)

....

....

3 Specify your preferred outcome

How do you want things to change? Make assertive and specific statements. You can change; just believe it!

....

....

4 Recognize the negative patterning involved

If you can do this, you are on your way. You are brave to have come this far. Deep self-hatred; the need to fill the emptiness inside; fear of anger; lack of trust; desire to be in control (ironic though it may seem); a need to punish yourself and a lack of self-forgiveness are some of the things that brought you here.

5 Change the negative patterns – re-pattern your life

We are all working on our negative patterning in our quest for personal development and self-esteem. Viewed in this way, we are all addicts – we are addicted to repeating patterns. Your addiction might actually be life-threatening or it might have the potential to wreck your life in a different way. It is impossible to compare the severity of addictions and their power to ruin lives. Each case is unique and only you know if you need professional assistance to help you to change your patterns. More and more people are recognizing their addictions and asking for help. There are numerous support groups available. Whatever your problem, remember that you are not alone. Go and find help if you need it.

You are a wonderfully brave and talented woman and all you really need is love – lots and lots of self-love.

Techniques for Change

Whether you need outside support or not, you will always need your own support. Use any of the techniques for change which will help you to boost your confidence and self-belief.

Self-Supporting Affirmations

- I am free.
- No person has any power over me.
- Nothing has any power over me.
- I am safe at all times.
- I can trust my instincts.
- I love myself.

- I forgive myself.
- I am decisive.
- I can make things happen.

As you say these affirmations, visualize their truth. See yourself free and happy, and make this vision as real as you can.

Try writing affirmations for a change. Take one affirmation and write it 20 times on one side of paper. If your negativity surfaces (as eventually it will if you repeat this exercise enough), write your negative thoughts on the other side of the paper. This is a powerful way to start releasing negativity. Don't give up on this exercise; it isn't just academic. Remember that positive affirmations can replace negative beliefs. Keep at it – your reward is your freedom!

Visualization: Letting Go

Read through the following visualization and then relax, close your eyes and enjoy the experience.

As you drift into relaxation, you find yourself in a lovely, tranquil place. Choose any beautiful outdoor environment that you prefer. Take some time to enjoy the details of the scene.

Someone is coming into view, and as she walks towards you, you see that it is your mother. As you watch her approach, she becomes smaller and smaller and before your eyes she becomes the tiny girl she once was a long time ago. She is laughing and jumping about, she is full of fun and wants to play. Watch her skipping about and enjoying herself, such a sweet and happy little girl. Suddenly she is no longer smiling; something has upset her and she is crying. She is very sad and you watch her sadness. Her mother and father come and comfort her and now she is smiling again as they all walk away together out of view.

As you are enjoying the beautiful scenery, someone else appears on the horizon and starts to walk towards you. You see that it is your father. As you watch him approach, he becomes smaller and smaller and before your eyes he becomes the tiny boy he once was years ago. He is tearing about and laughing, he is full of fun and wants to play. You watch him running around; what a sweet and carefree little boy. And then he is not laughing any more; he is miserable, something has upset him and he is crying. He is very sad and you watch his sadness. His mother and father come and comfort him and now he is smiling again as they walk away together.

Visualize yourself as a little girl again. Now you too are playing in this beautiful and tranquil place. And as you are watching yourself, so happy and carefree, you hear laughter and see those two other small children running towards you. You come together and join hands in a circle and you are all laughing as you go round and round. Let these children play together for a while.

And now the children have gone and there are three adults in their place. You see yourself and your mother and your father holding hands and laughing as you go round and round. You are happy together. Watch the three of you enjoying being with each other.

When you are ready, dissolve the picture and return from the visualization.

> *There are always more opportunities to get it right, to fashion our lives in the ways we deserve to have them. Don't waste your time hating a failure. Failure is a greater teacher than success. Listen, learn, go on.*
>
> (CLARISSA PINKOLA ESTÉS,
> WOMEN WHO RUN WITH THE WOLVES)

Listen, learn, *forgive* and go on.

Women as Mothers

*How is it that mothers can be regarded
by so many people as both angel and
villain, chaste vessel of purity and whore,
queen of wisdom and consummate idiot?*

(CLAIRE RAYNER, 'YOU CAN'T HAVE IT ALL',
SUNDAY TIMES JUNE 11 1995)

'Women as mothers' the very words plunge me into so many emotional states that I don't know quite where to begin.

As a mother, I know only too well that well-meaning and helpful advice about 'how to parent' is always inappropriate, and so this chapter will take a different approach. We are the mothers we have learned to be: our belief, behaviour and emotional patterns create our own unique brand of mothering. However, we do share the experience of some powerfully strong cultural beliefs which contain variations on the following themes.

- Mothers love their children.
- Women are born to be mothers.
- Motherhood is natural and easy.
- Mother knows best.
- Motherhood is bliss.
- Motherhood is instinctive.

What sort of things did you believe about motherhood before you had your baby?

Those who have chosen not to have any children know only too well about the silent pressures imposed by our society on a woman who 'contravenes' the cultural imperatives. Those who cannot have children suffer their own individual agonies. And those of us who choose to have children begin a relationship of incredible complexity from the moment of our first child's conception.

Whether you are a single parent, in a nuclear family or living in a commune, motherhood is really all about getting to know a new part of yourself as well as getting to know your child. Eighteen years ago I walked in the pouring rain down a country lane to a phone box to find out if my pregnancy test was positive. I remember that I was excited and nervous, but as if it were yesterday I can still feel the awareness which overwhelmed me – if I was pregnant, then I would never be really on my own ever again. As I left the phone box, thrilled by my exciting news, I knew that I had begun a relationship which would last all of my life and that in the gaining of so much I had also lost something. Already a little seed of guilt was sown!

MOTHERHOOD AND SELF-ESTEEM

These two concepts are uncomfortable bedfellows; why do they sit so uneasily with each other?

Motherhood is a fast-moving and ever-changing experience which never seems to settle into a recognizable and controllable routine. Once we can reconcile ourselves to this emotional roller-coaster ride, we can begin to enjoy the adventure, but we need to remember to hang on to our self-esteem.

Figure 1 on page 2 shows how any experience can be seen as the coming together of our whole selves (mind, body, spirit and

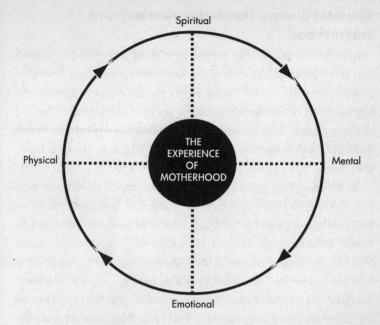

Figure 17 Motherhood from a holistic perspective

emotions). Figure 17 looks at the experience of motherhood in this context.

Our spiritual, mental, emotional and physical elements are mutually dependent: they interact with each other to create balance, harmony and self-esteem, or imbalance, discord and low self-esteem. Any experience can be viewed in this way; we bring our whole selves to each of our life experiences. The quality of our experiences depends upon the balance (or imbalance) of our interacting energies. Motherhood imposes its own special difficulties upon this delicate balancing act. Let's look at our spiritual, mental, emotional and physical energies within the context of our mothering to see why this should be so.

Spiritual Energy (Inner Awareness) and Motherhood

Our individual spirituality means something quite unique to each one of us. Spiritual experience is here understood as a feeling of connection with the life force: when we are connecting with the spiritual part of our being, we feel a sense of belonging to the rest of the universe. This feeling is one of heightened intuitive awareness and its development requires that we look at our own inner development as opposed to our worldly progress.

In terms of our spiritual development, motherhood can be a paradox. Again, it is important to remember that each one of us has a unique experience of being a mother (and that this can be totally different with each of our children – to add to the complexity). In spite of our own individual experiences, I think it is true to say that we can all relate to this paradox. On the one hand we have the image of the 'radiant mother', and on the other all the more mundane experiences of our role. Motherhood can offer the experience of divinity (if only for a fleeting moment). Some women experience their pregnancies in a very spiritual way, and they love being pregnant because they feel close to mother earth; other women just feel ill! Some mothers have wonderful natural births where they feel at one with the universe; others have frightening experiences and need all the drugs and modern technology available. The potential for a great spiritual experience seems to be on offer, but many of us don't reach these radiant heights (and if we do, they don't last long). It is easy to see why motherhood and guilt are often so closely related (right from the very start).

Moving on from our birthing into our early motherhood, we find ourselves in a job for which we have no experience (except our own experience of being mothered). Modern society isolates us in a new and exhausting role with no time off, no holidays and no pay: it is difficult to maintain a calm, spiritual centre under such conditions (even though we love the baby so much). And what if we don't love our baby? The pressures may be too great and we just crack: we cannot give to our baby (and all the rest of our needy family) because we just have nothing left to give. And as if this pain were not enough, we add to the burden by feeling that we have failed and so our self-esteem hits rock-bottom.

Spiritual balance is very important in these days of self-doubt, guilt and fatigue, but the irony is that we need time for self-nurturing and spiritual development, and time for ourselves is now something that we no longer have. We need to recognize our own inner needs at this time and take any free moments just to sit and be. Remember that perfect mothering is a myth and that a clear mind and a centred heart are more important than a hoovered floor! We cannot nurture others if we are not nurturing ourselves. Meditation, relaxation, listening to music, a walk in the country – do whatever you need to maintain your spiritual connection and your self-esteem.

Mental Energy (Understanding) and Motherhood

We understand a situation by using our mental energy. The type of thoughts we have in adulthood will depend upon the basic beliefs we learned as small children. We have seen how negative self-beliefs affect the quality of our lives. We have looked at the process of changing self-beliefs by using affirmations and visualizations and we will need to use these techniques over and over once we become mothers. Motherhood is an incredible challenger of self-belief. We are required to maintain our self-esteem when we feel that we are 'not a good enough mother'; when we feel that we are a failure; when we feel resentful, tired, angry, unloving, noncaring... The burden of trying to be a perfect mother is intolerable.

As mothers, we are confronted with our negative beliefs about ourselves and our world as well as the popular cultural myths about womanhood and motherhood – a tangled web of family and cultural patterning. Look at this fundamental contradictory belief: *a mother has a powerful role/motherhood is not important.*

- Children who are well-mothered become balanced adults with high self-esteem who know how to make a success of their lives. (The hand that rocks the cradle rules the world.)

- 'Good mothers' who stay at home to look after their children are doing boring and mundane work. (I am/she is 'just' a mother/housewife.)

No wonder we get confused. If we have such an important role, how come we have so little status?

We need to look carefully at our ideas surrounding motherhood. Many of the beliefs which increase our low self-esteem have no foundation in reality unless we ourselves perpetuate them. Recognize what the job of mothering means to you and validate and support yourself at all times, even when (in fact, especially when) you make mistakes. Respect yourself for the wonderful job you are doing and your children will reflect these feelings of respect (and so the job gets easier).

Emotional Energy (Feelings) and Motherhood

> *Children have much more trust in humanness than they do in sainthood and perfection.*
>
> (VIRGINIA SATIR, *PEOPLEMAKING*)

And so here we find ourselves with a job description which we can never fulfil: just as we get the hang of a particular role, the job requirements change. Our concept of self changes because we are responsible for another human being. This responsibility can bring an amazing sense of well-being and purpose and/or feelings of loss, low self-esteem and lack of direction. Yes, it is possible to experience such conflicting emotions. We can feel utterly different from one moment to the next. Alongside this very understandable emotional turbulence runs our own particular assortment of ideas and beliefs about motherhood. Underlying your own beliefs and connecting you with all other mothers of our cultural tradition lies a (largely) unmentionable emotional area.

Emotional balance requires that we are able to get in touch with our feelings and to express them appropriately. This can be hard at the very best of times; it sometimes feels impossible for a mother. How is it possible to be the self-sacrificial mother on the one hand, while feeling anger, resentment and guilt on the other? When these feelings start to emerge we suppress them – they really are most unworthy and not nice! Even if we find ourselves in a group of other mothers who are willing to share their true feelings, there is still a residual guilt which follows us home. Motherhood is a state of conflict, and until we recognize this reality, we will be unreal and unhappy in our mothering role.

- We can resent our child's dependency while being afraid of their independence.
- We can feel overwhelmed by our child's need for attention and then lost and unloved when the child accepts the attention of others.

Motherhood is a truly amazing and miraculous experience, but it is not bliss. Being a mother can take us to the heights of love and the depths of anger and resentment. All mothers ride this roller-coaster, and when we can accept this more readily, our self-esteem will no longer be on the line. You are not an unworthy mother if your feelings are less than saintly. Our children are humans too and they can relate to our humanness. Perfection is not part of the job description because perfect mothering does not exist. The best we can do is the best we can do! The honest and appropriate expression of the feelings that we least admire in ourselves is a fantastic way to liberation. Only we can free ourselves from the self-imposed and culturally supported chains of motherhood. Let yourself off that big hook of guilt and do yourself and your children the biggest favour you can – be real with your children and they can be real with you.

Physical Energy (Behaviour) and Motherhood

These are just a few women's comments about motherhood.

- I vowed that I would never physically abuse my child and then last week I got so mad I slapped him hard and now I feel so terrible and I can never make it up to him.

- I always try to let my children make their own decisions about things and then if they make mistakes they learn for themselves the hard way. I don't think that children respond to discipline, they have to find out for themselves.

- We have strict rules in our house, I think kids need to know how far they can go or they just keep pushing further and further.

- A short, sharp, smack never did anyone any harm and sometimes my children just ask for it. I can't stand an atmosphere over anything, I'd rather give them a smack and then at least it's all over.

- I'm never sure when to say 'yes' and when to say 'no' and this is getting harder as they are growing up. Sometimes I agree to them doing something and then I spend the whole day worrying about them. They have a good time and I'm a wreck.

We all do this job differently according to our own thought, feeling and behaviour patterns, and what is 'right' for one mother will be 'wrong' for another. However, certain behaviours are more nurturing than others and we will be looking again at the 'nurturing' family later in this chapter.

Given the complexities of the job and of our own patterns, however can we tell if we are doing the best for our children? Always start with yourself. If you are feeling balanced and high in self-esteem, you will be confident to make decisions and to follow them through with appropriate action. If you are low in self-esteem, then you cannot trust your own judgement and your decision-making and action-taking will be ineffective and inconsistent. You will know when you feel like this because you will feel victimized by your family.

Victim consciousness denotes the need for a change in mothering behaviour. Teenagers are great at pushing our victim buttons.

- Oh, why can't I go, all the others are going?
- I really need to take the car tonight, otherwise I will miss this really important (whatever).
- There's no point going if I can't stay out until... All the others are allowed.

And so they go on trying to change the rules and widening the boundaries, day after day it sometimes seems. Each time you are confronted in this way, ask yourself this question: 'If I say yes, how will I feel?'

If you will feel unsure, worried and low in self-esteem, you are allowing yourself to be victimized. Support your own instincts; learn to say 'no' when you want to (you might need to practice this); investigate what is going on (what about all these 'others'? A quick phone call to the parents of 'the others' will often reveal a different picture from the one you have been given). Don't be afraid to be an assertive mother; your children can only benefit.

Don't allow your children to victimize you. It is in neither their best interest nor yours. You deserve to be treated with respect and your children will only respect you if you respect yourself. Remember that children do what we do and not what we say.

High and low self-esteem are contagious and your children will catch whatever variety you have. Work on yourself and all the rest will follow. Recognize and accept your guilt, anger, resentment etc, then you can let these feelings go and move on to clear and assertive decision-making and action-taking.

When we are high in self-esteem, we treat ourselves and others with respect. As we value ourselves, so we can value others. Children respond to positive action and supportive parenting which enhances their own self-esteem: when there is mutual respect within the family, everyone feels self-respect so there is mutual self-esteem.

WOMEN AS DAUGHTERS/WOMEN AS MOTHERS

We learned our deep beliefs about mothering when we were baby daughters, and we learned them from our mothers. We can make a direct link with the patterns we have learned and the ones that we are now teaching our own children.

EXERCISE:
Memories of My Mother

Go back as far as you can into your childhood to answer these questions. It may be helpful to look at some photos of yourself and your mother taken in those early days. Perhaps you can remember some specific outings, holidays or events that will help you to focus your memories. If you can talk to your mother about your babyhood, so much the better.

1 Was your mother very emotional during your childhood?
Yes/No

2 If the answer is 'yes', describe her emotions and the ways that she showed them:

....

3 Was your mother able to show her love for you?　　Yes/No

4 If *'yes'*, describe the ways that she demonstrated her love – if 'no', say why you think she could not show you her love:

....

5 Describe how you are feeling now, as you are doing this exercise:

....

6 Do you think that your mother enjoyed looking after you when you were a child?　　　　　　　　　　　　Yes/No

7 Explain why you think she did or did not enjoy looking after you:

....

8 How would you describe the relationship between your parents when you were small? In which ways do you think they were supportive or not supportive of each other:

....

9 How would you describe your mother's levels of self-esteem when you were a little girl? (If you can ask her now how she felt it might be helpful.)

....

10 Why do you think that she felt this way?

....

11 Describe your relationship with your mother now

....

(If she is dead, you can still answer because you will always have a relationship with your mother.)

Some of you may have found this exercise very painful. Mother and child relationships are always potentially highly charged emotionally. We begin this emotional roller-coaster ride as soon as we are born. When we ourselves become mothers, we take a front seat and the speed accelerates. Because of the natural turbulence involved in the mother/child relationship, it is important that we hold on to our self-respect, otherwise fear and guilt (and other assorted emotions) can lead us into victim behaviour, self-doubt and low self-esteem.

EXERCISE:
Me as a Mother

In this exercise we change roles, from daughter to mother.

1 Are you able to show your emotions to your children?

Yes/No

2 If not, why not? If you are able to show your emotions, how do you do this?

....

3 Do you find it easy to show physical affection for your children?　　　　　　　　　　　　　　　　**Yes/No**

4 In what ways do you show your love for your children?

....

5 Do you ever wish that you had not had your children? Yes/No

6 How would you describe the relationship between you and the father of your child (children)?

....

....

7 How do you think your role as a mother affects your levels of self-esteem?

....

....

8 Describe your relationship with your own children now:

....

....

Compare your answers with the ones you gave in the previous exercise. Can you see any connections?

Forgiving Our Parents; Forgiving Ourselves

As we unravel this patterning, it is very important to remember that our mothers had mothers too! Throughout this book there has been an ongoing and vital therapeutic theme; *remember that our parents had parents too!* The more work you can do on forgiving your parents, the easier it is to let go of your learned negative patterning. However, at this stage, where we are looking at our *own* role as a parent, this forgiveness of our own parents becomes absolutely vital. Suddenly (or so it seems) we are the grown-ups. We can rant and rave at our own parents' mistakes and then, before we know it, the roles have changed and our children are looking at us. If we cannot forgive our parents, then we cannot forgive ourselves, and guilt, pain and low self-esteem will accompany our motherhood. When we can clearly recognize that our parents were only passing on their patterns, then we can start to let go of those patterns ourselves. We can only ever teach what we know, we cannot teach what we don't know. This seems so very obvious but often it is hard to remember when we are looking at our own negative patterning. If we have been severely damaged emotionally and we discover the childhood roots of this damage, it can sometimes feel very difficult to remember that our parents were only working from their unconscious patterns.

Self-forgiveness is the link which allows motherhood and self-esteem to co-exist. The degree to which you can forgive your own mother and father is the degree to which you can forgive yourself. Yes, I have made so many mistakes as a mother: I continue to make them every day because in the motherhood game the rules keep changing. I sometimes look back and think that if only I had known this stuff about patterns, parents, forgiveness, guilt and self-esteem all those years ago, then I could have been a better mother – and before I know it, I'm back on the guilt trail.

It is never too late to change our patterns, and as we do so, this automatically affects our children (however grown up they are, however far away they are). Recognize your parents' patterns; recognize your own patterns; change your own patterns and your children will be free to change. We pass on our patterns to our children – let them be patterns of high self-esteem.

MOTHERHOOD AND THE NURTURING FAMILY

We have previously looked at the concepts of the nurturing family and the troubled family in relation to our own upbringing. Look back to Figure 16 on page 116 to see the range of behaviours and feelings experienced within the nurturing and the troubled families. How do the behaviours and feelings demonstrated in the diagram relate to the family in which you are now the mother?

Let's be clear about the nature of family life. It is a minefield of possible emotional conflict and all members of the family will make mistakes. The nurturing family recognizes this important reality and knows that validation and support create loving, committed relationships and high self-esteem. It is not always easy to maintain good open communication especially if you are feeling stretched in your mothering role. All too often we have to implement unpopular rules and regulations in order to keep the family show running. Sometimes there is just no time for a lengthy explanation; it really is just a case of do it 'because I said so'. We don't always feel positive, and we would sometimes like to walk away from this very difficult job. We can't always freely express our feelings; we may need to withdraw emotionally from our loved ones in order to get ourselves together. Members of the nurturing family allow for difficulties and are able to support their members through the hard times.

One of the criteria for the nurturing family is a good supportive relationship between parents. This does not mean that you cannot mother a nurturing family unless you are happily married. Many women are bringing up their families single-handed and others have remarried and created mixed families. All families have problems, but it's the way that we deal with them that differentiates between the nurturing and the troubled family. It is entirely possible for separated parents to continue to give each other emotional support in the upbringing of their children. There will be problems to face for the children of separated parents, but this can be done with the help and support of both parents. A good (but difficult) job can be done by a single mother without support who is working on changing her own patterns and creating self-esteem. Where re-marriage has occurred, the quality of family life will depend on the relationships between all those involved (step-parents; ex-husbands;

ex-wives; step-siblings; step-grandparents). This will most probably be a complicated situation, but it will always be potentially nurturing if the lines of communication between all parties are kept open and feelings are shared.

Whatever your situation, the quality of your mothering will always depend on your own levels of self-esteem. Respect yourself for the wonderful job that you are doing and let yourself off the hook of guilt. When you are free of guilt, you liberate your children to be themselves. Good communication, trust and openness, follow. You and your children (as they grow up) each have your own difficult patterns, but these can be changed – family life can be a supportive and hopeful affair where there is mutual respect and self-esteem.

EXERCISE:
Applying the Five-Step Programme for Change

Choose a particular area of your mothering that is causing you problems at the moment

1 Assess the situation
Describe the problem.

....

....

2 Decide what you would like to change
What in particular don't you like about this situation? Take no notice of any feelings about the impossibility of being able to make changes.

....

....

3 Specify your preferred outcome

State exactly how you want things to change. What is it that you want for yourself in this situation? Be creative and know that you can change your life.

....

....

4 Recognize the negative patterning involved

Think long and hard about the beliefs that may have created this situation. Was there a link between the answers to the two exercises 'Memories of my mother' and 'Me as a mother'?

....

....

5 Change the negative patterns – re-pattern your life

How balanced are your spiritual, mental, emotional and physical energies? Are you a victim as well as a mother? Who is victimizing you and how? Why are you allowing yourself to be victimized? Allow yourself to be different, take the risk and change; there is everything to gain. If motherhood feels like a victim role, then you have low self-esteem and you are allowing your family to treat you badly. The popular role of self-sacrificial mother will never allow children to develop self-respect and self-worth. Letting your children 'get away' with poor behaviour ensures the continuation of negative patterning and low self-belief within your family. How can children feel self-esteem if they are allowed to treat their own mother badly? The licence to victimize parents sits uneasily on the shoulders of young people and the family is a troubled one where self-esteem is at rock bottom.

Use any of the techniques for change which are appropriate – and then *change*! Wherever you lead, your children will follow.

Work on your own self-esteem and then they will know how to develop their own.

KEY POINTS TO REMEMBER

We have touched very briefly upon many issues in this chapter. Motherhood is a hugely challenging area and sometimes it helps to remember a few vital key points which will always be applicable.

- Motherhood is a *big job*.
- I am a good mother. I am doing my best.
- Motherhood is vital – the survival of the race depends upon it.
- Guilt is not an intrinsic part of motherhood. I don't *have* to feel guilty.
- When guilt engulfs me, I can just step out of it. Guilt ruins family life.
- I need to look after myself. I cannot give to others if I have nothing left to give.
- There are no perfect mothers; we all make lots of mistakes.
- It's OK to make mistakes; this is how we learn.
- I am free to feel and to express all of my emotions.
- Motherhood is a state of potential conflict. I can accept this and work with it. I am flexible and creative.
- My children do what I do and not what I say.
- I forgive and thank my mother. She taught me what she knew about mothering.
- It is safe for my children to grow up. I can easily let them go.
- I pass on my patterns of self-esteem to my children. I can create high self-esteem.
- I deserve a supportive and validating family life.

7

Women in the Workplace

Our society rates paid employment higher than any other form of work and those of us who are caring for families or are unable to find employment are highly likely to be affected by these cultural values. And if we leave the kitchen (so to speak) to enter the world of work, we will face many traditional male prejudices as well as the problem of who does what in the kitchen when we are not there!

The good news is that more and more women are finding their place in the world of work. It can be done, and we can have a meaningful career as well as a family if that is what we really want.

We do need to be clear about why and how we do the things we do. If we are motivated by unconscious cultural and family patterns, we may be doing things in ways that do not support high self-esteem. Each one of us has different needs and it is important that we recognize and fulfil these needs, otherwise we will be low in self-esteem. One woman may stay at home to look after her family and feel satisfied that she is doing an important and worthwhile job, while another woman might feel totally trapped and limited by the experience. There is no question of who is 'right' or 'wrong' in this situation. This is not a question of morality but one of differences.

We encountered large dollops of guilt in the chapter on mothering and we can see them again here. Leave other people's opinions about what you 'should' and 'shouldn't' be doing out of the picture. Guilt lowers self-esteem. When we are low in self-esteem, it is hard to trust our own judgement and our own decision-making powers. Abandon guilt and look to your own needs. When your needs are fulfilled, you are able to give of your best to others (in the home or outside of it) and you will feel high in self-esteem. Do you gain satisfaction from the ways in which you spend your time? The following exercise will help you to look at why you do the things you do.

EXERCISE:
Your Work and Why You Do It

Are you at home looking after a family? Are you a mother who also works outside the home? Are you unemployed and single or with a partner? Are you in some other different circumstances?

1 Describe your circumstances:

....

2 Describe the type of work that you do each day, both paid and unpaid tasks:

....

3 Do you enjoy your daily tasks?   Yes/No

4 Explain why you do/do not enjoy your daily tasks:

....

....

5 Do you see the value in the work you do?   Yes/No

6 Explain why you value/don't value your work:

....

....

7 How do you feel that your work is valued by society?

....

....

8 Does your work bring you satisfaction?　　　　　　**Yes/No**

9 If not, describe why it doesn't. If it does, describe why it does:

....

....

Review your answers. Are you happy with your circumstances or would you like to change them? Is there anything that you could do to improve your situation? Are you doing things that you don't want to do? Are you not doing things that you would like to do? Why is it difficult to make changes?

WOMEN IN UNPAID EMPLOYMENT

If you have been out of paid work for a while, you may be suffering from some loss of identity. When we are working for money we often define ourselves in terms of the job we do: 'I'm a care worker'; 'I'm a doctor'; 'I'm a shop assistant'; 'I'm a teacher' and so on. When we are no longer out at work, we lose this part of our identity and we may find ourselves described only in terms of our relationship with others – as someone's mother, wife or daughter. We may even start to define ourselves in this way. During those years when I stayed at home to look after my young family, I remember my own confused feelings about my role. One day

I was the earth mother and I recognized the importance of my role in the great scheme of things; the next day I was 'just a boring housewife and mother'. The culturally created ambivalence of motherhood constantly leads mothers to question the validity of their role.

Women who are trying to return to work after bringing up their families often face a severe crisis of confidence. The world of work can feel very threatening. We have seen how the experience of family life can constantly challenge our self-esteem. Even if our partners and children were always supporting and validating our role, this would still not be enough. In our society the unpaid domestic worker receives no cultural accolade and it is difficult to maintain high self-esteem when the job is so undervalued. Financial dependency also affects the way we feel about ourselves. Some women have no money to spend on themselves. If we have to rely on our partner or the state for every penny we spend, then we lose our sense of being able to provide for ourselves. However loving, generous and understanding our partner, this lack of financial independence can affect our levels of self-esteem.

We are all in different situations. Some women will already be in the workplace and encountering different problems and we will be looking at this issue shortly. The following exercise is for women who are thinking about entering or re-entering the world of work.

EXERCISE:
Entering Paid Employment

1 **How do you feel about going out to work? Describe all the emotions involved:**

....

....

2 Will you have to change your domestic arrangements so that you can go to work?   Yes/No

3 If the answer is yes, how will you make these changes?

....

....

4 Will you need the support of other family members?   Yes/No

5 If yes, can you be sure of their support? Describe the type of support that you will need:

....

....

6 What type of work are you interested in?

....

....

7 Do you need some more qualifications or training to do your preferred job?   Yes/No

8 If so, how do you feel about taking the necessary courses?

....

....

9 Review your answers. Are there any practical or emotional issues that might stand in your way?   Yes/No

10 If so, describe what you think they are:

....

....

WOMEN AT WORK

For all of us, whether single, with partners, with or without children, there is a potential set of problems to face just because we are women. Traditionally the world of work has been peopled largely by men. Women who worked usually did so either in a capacity which supported male bosses (PA, secretary, typist etc) or in a role which was clearly designated as women's work (nurse, care assistant, cleaner etc). The times have changed and women have fought for their freedom in the workplace. It is possible for us to climb to the very top of our profession, but we may encounter much resistance along the way.

We often hear of cases where men have treated women as less than equal in the workplace and many of us have experienced this behaviour. It is easy to understand how men can feel so threatened by us and also easy to recognize that their bad behaviour stems from old-fashioned beliefs about the roles of men and women in our society. It is harder to understand the animosity and bad behaviour of *women* towards other women in the workplace. Yes, it is true, women do not always operate as 'sisters' in the workplace. This is not a very popular line, but we must look at this issue if we are to understand our own cultural and family patterns. I have heard so many women say that they would prefer to work for a man. When questioned, the issue does not usually revolve around the professional ability of the woman (who has had to work *extra* hard for that promotion). No, the problems lie in old-fashioned beliefs about the roles of men and women which are held by *women*.

EXERCISE:

Behaviour in the Workplace

1 Do you feel that you have been, or are being, unfairly treated in the workplace?   Yes/No

2 If you do, explain the circumstances:

....

....

3 Do you think that you were treated badly because you are a woman?   Yes/No

4 If so, explain how this happened:

....

....

5 How did you respond to the unfair treatment?

....

....

6 Have you ever been in a situation where you have been unable to stand up for yourself for fear of losing your job?
                                                                                                                   Yes/No

7 If so, describe the circumstances:

....

....

8 Have you ever been sexually harassed by a man in the workplace?   Yes/No

9 If so, what happened and how did you act?

....

....

10 Do you like working with other women?   Yes/No

11 Have you ever been badly treated by women in the
    workplace?   Yes/No

12 If so, describe what happened:

....

....

13 Do you think that your promotion prospects have ever been
    affected because you are a woman?   Yes/No

14 If so, explain how this has become evident:

....

....

15 If you are being treated badly at work, do you thinkthat
    there is anything that you can do about it?   Yes/No

Male and Female Energies in the Workplace

Each of us, of course, will have our own unique experiences
within the workplace, but whatever our situation, the most
important quality we need to take to work is our self-esteem.
Being successful in the workplace requires that we bring together
our inspirational feminine energy and our action-planning, go-
getting masculine energy. Traditionally women have taken the

more passive and receptive roles within relationships. This is changing and in particular it is changing in the world of work. Let's look at the qualities of our inner female and inner male energies (taken from Figure 10 on page 36).

Going out to work for money requires the development of our inner male energies. Look at Table 2 and think about your own strengths and weaknesses. Are you able to assert your own masculine energies? If not, you will be out of balance and low in self-esteem and you will find yourself victimized in the workplace.

Table 2

Inner male energy	Inner female energy
Rational	Emotional
Active	Intuitive
Logical	Nurturing
Risk-taking	Reflective
Conceptual	Instinctive
Thinking	Inward-looking
Assertive	Receptive
Externalizing	Internalizing
Outgoing	Visionary
Goal-orientated	Spiritual
Planning	Sensitive
Physical	Wise

Review your answers to the previous exercise, 'Behaviour in the workplace'. While some of the bad behaviour which we encounter in the workplace may be the result of pure sexual discrimination, most will have more to do with our own personal behavioural style. We do not *have* to be victims in the workplace just because we are women. If you are suffering from sexual harassment or discrimination, then it is important that you act in some way. Be sure to keep careful written and dated documentation of any conversations which could be useful as evidence if you are planning to make an official complaint. You always have choices; you can leave, complain or put up with the behaviour. Whatever you decide will depend upon the type of behaviour you are encountering and your own personal circumstances. A woman with self-esteem respects her own needs and is not afraid to make informed decisions and choices. If the situation at work is serious and cannot be changed, then you need to think about the possibility of leaving, with your self-esteem intact. If your circumstances are less critical, then it is very likely that you can change the way that you are being treated by changing your own behaviour.

AGGRESSIVE, SUBMISSIVE AND ASSERTIVE BEHAVIOUR

It's not what you do, it's the way that you do it that determines the nature of your outcome. Think about the ways that you behave in any situation (in or out of work). Figure 18 demonstrates the range of behaviour which is available to us during our social interactions. The nature of our behaviour and our levels of self-esteem are directly linked. When we are low in self-esteem, we act as victims and allow people to walk all over us while we become angry, resentful and blaming. When we are high in self-esteem, we respect our own needs and recognize the wishes of others; we know what we want and are not afraid to go out and get it.

We can only get what we want if we know what we want and are able to communicate our needs to other people. Assertive (non-victim) behaviour requires that we develop and use good communication skills. Can you express your needs clearly to others? Can you say 'no' when you need to? Are you ready to go out there and make things happen? Are you ready to take

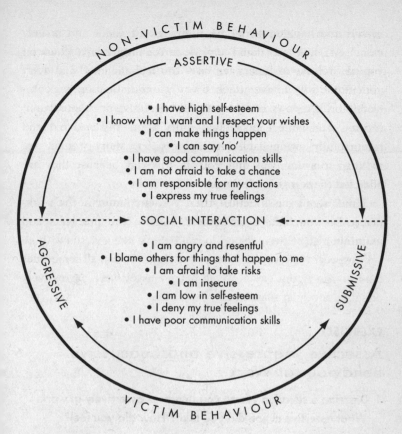

Figure 18 Types of behaviour

responsibility for your decisions and actions? If you find it difficult to be assertive, you will probably be behaving like a victim. Figure 18 shows a two-way arrow between aggressive and submissive behaviour because in victim mode we swing between these extremes.

Imagine that you and I are having a conversation and you say something which hurts me. I feel threatened by you and so I withdraw and become submissive (silently feeling sorry for myself and hanging on to my unexpressed anger and resentment). At some later date I explode into an aggressive attack on you and release my angry feelings. You feel alienated and don't understand why I have attacked you. Communication has completely broken down and you may be aggressive or submissive in return. Meanwhile I am feeling guilty about my outburst and remorsefully swing back into submission. Many women are inclined to swing back and forth in this way because they are addicted to their guilty feelings!

Think about the difficulties that you encounter in the workplace. Do you behave assertively, resolve the problems and maintain high self-esteem, or do you behave like a victim with no self-respect? However high our self-esteem, we can all sometimes fall into the victim mode. We all behave assertively, aggressively or submissively at some time.

EXERCISE:

Assertive, Aggressive and Submissive Behaviour at Work

1 **Describe a situation where you behaved assertively at work. What assertive action did you take? How did you feel?**

....

....

2 **What was the outcome of your action?**

....

....

3 **Describe a time when you behaved aggressively at work. How did you feel?**

....

4 What was the outcome?

....

....

5 Now think of a time when you behaved submissively at work. What did you do? How did you feel?

....

....

6 What was the outcome?

....

....

If you are being victimized in the workplace, look carefully at the situation. If there is absolutely nothing you can do to change your circumstances, then you can always leave. However, amazing things can happen when we change our behaviour and stop acting like a victim (victims attract bullies). Start to develop assertiveness techniques. Recognize your areas of vulnerability, where you are inclined to allow others to use you as a doormat. Recognize your strengths and use them to their full advantage. Replace your negative thought, feeling and behaviour patterns with positively affirming success patterns. Success creates success, positivity attracts positivity and self-esteem creates more self-esteem.

EXERCISE:
Applying the Five-Step Programme for Change

You may be trying to start work for the first time and facing your own personal barriers. You might be trying to re-enter the world of work and be struggling with self-esteem and/or practical issues. Or you may already be there, facing difficulties within the workplace. Choose your own particular problem area.

1 Assess the situation
Describe the problem.

....

....

2 Decide what you would like to change
Know that you *can* change.

....

....

3 Specify your preferred outcome
Be as precise as possible and visualize your outcome.

....

....

4 Recognize the negative patterning involved
Are your own deep beliefs coloured by the cultural view of traditional male and female roles?

....

....

Look particularly at developing the energies of your inner male. Women who balance their intuitive and emotional capacities with their decision-making and action-planning abilities can create happiness and success in the workplace.

TRADITIONAL PATRIARCHAL SOCIETY

Our traditional patriarchal society has a lot to answer for. Over the centuries women have been disempowered and marginalized by a culture which elevates masculine energy (mental and physical) and denigrates feminine energy (emotional and spiritual). Our society has been out of balance. Reason, logic and action-planning (particularly financial planning) have created today's materialistic society. Spiritual and emotional matters have been given little credibility, and the emphasis has been on using mind and force to 'conquer' the natural world in pursuit of money and power. When we look at the state of our planet today, we can see that our imbalanced activity has created an exactly corresponding imbalance in the natural world.

To reach our highest potential, we each need to balance all our energies – spiritual and emotional (female energy), and mental and physical (male energy). When we can create this inner balance, we will make real changes out in the world. We have created imbalance in our planet because we are individually out of balance. As each person works towards balancing their own male and female energy, the planet will reflect this change.

Men are not to blame for the oppression of women. No one is to blame. We have undergone a cycle of spiritual and emotional repression and both men and women have been affected. The cycle of imbalance did not work; the planet is wounded and so are its female and male inhabitants. The powers of the feminine are on the rise, and the energy of the universe is seeking balance.

So what has this to do with women in the workplace? Well, it has everything to do with it. To be high in self-esteem with our energy flowing freely, we need to balance our male and female energies. Our cultural and family patterning has enabled us all to subscribe to the myth that men personify male energy and women personify female energy. Thought and action have been considered high status activities, while emotional and spiritual sensitivity have been largely disregarded. So both women and men have suffered. Men have come to symbolize male energy (intellectual, assertive and outward-looking) and have lost touch with their inner awareness and sensitivity. Women have come to symbolize female energy (sensitive, nurturing and receptive) and have lost touch with their ability to act directly and assertively in the world.

Our culture is changing as the pendulum swings towards feminine energy. There has been a great revival in interest in spiritual and emotional matters, and as the power of the feminine rises, it is being reflected in the workplace. Women are taking powerful positions in the world of work because they are recognizing their inner female power and simultaneously developing their own inner male energy.

Conclusion

A Woman with Self-Esteem

When women come to my self-esteem workshops, I know that they have *already started* to create self-esteem in their lives because they take themselves seriously enough to come. Similarly, when you bought this book, you were expressing the belief that you deserved self-esteem, and so you had already taken that most important first step.

There are those who:

- don't know and don't know they don't know;
- don't know and know they don't know;
- know they don't know and try to find out;
- find out and change.

Because you are looking to change, you will find the ways to do so. You are an amazing woman with all the inner qualities which allow you to experience your womanhood as an empowering and creative process.

Creative consciousness is the awareness that we can locate our own personal power to make effective decisions to create our desired outcomes. We have seen how self-awareness creates self-esteem and how becoming aware requires that we look back into our past to see where we have come from. As we examine the ways that we have been influenced by our family and cultural patterns, we will face some amazing (and sometimes painful) discoveries about ourselves and our loved ones. As we unravel the threads of our own unique patterning, we will begin to understand why we do the things we do and how we can effect change in our lives.

This book has addressed some difficult issues which are not easy to face. All of our negative patterning is addictive until we can recognize it and change it, and addictions bring disempowerment, anger and low self-esteem. It is easy to become caught in the negative spiral of victim consciousness where we blame someone for our feelings of oppression. But blame, disempowerment and low self-esteem go hand-in-hand to create a life of depression, low energy and negativity, and these patterns are passed on to our children to act out all over again!

Once we have understood the energetic dynamics involved in the creation of our lives, we have two choices. We can choose to live with our negative patterns and low self-esteem and to pass these on to our children, or we can change our negative patterning and become high in self-esteem and pass this on to our children. There really is no choice.

You are strong and powerful. Embrace your power, create the reality you truly desire and become a woman with self-esteem.

References and Further Reading

Bamford, Caroline, & McCarthy, Catherine (eds.), *Women Mean Business,* BBC Books, 1991.

Conran, Shirley, *Lace,* Penguin Books, 1982.

Estés, Clarissa Pinkola, *Women Who Run with the Wolves,* Rider, 1993.

Field, Lynda, *Creating Self-Esteem,* Vermilion, 2001.

Field, Lynda, *The Self-Esteem Workbook,* Vermilion, 2001.

Gawain, Shakti, *Living in the Light,* Eden Grove Editions, 1988.

Gawain, Shakti, *Creative Visualization,* Bantam Books, 1987.

Hay, Louise, *You Can Heal Your Life,* Eden Grove Editions, 1988.

Hay, Louise, *Love Yourself Heal Your Life Workbook,* Eden Grove Editions, 1990.

Norwood, Robin, *Women Who Love Too Much,* Arrow Books, 1985.

Roman, Sanaya, *Personal Power Through Awareness,* H.J. Kramer Inc., 1986.

Roman, Sanaya, *Spiritual Growth,* H.J. Kramer Inc., 1989.

Satir, Virginia, *Peoplemaking,* Souvenir Press, 1978.

Useful Addresses

AUSTRALIA/NEW ZEALAND
The Compassionate Friends
79 Stirling Street, Perth, Western
Australia 6000
Tel 09 227 5698

Samaritan Befrienders
60 Bagot Road, Subiaco, Western
Australia 6008
Tel 381 5555 Fax 388 2368

UNIFAM
262 Pitt Street, Sydney 2000
Tel 02 261 4077 Fax 02 261 3255

Women with Eating Disorders Resource
Centre
Room 111, Cranmer Centre, PO Box
4520, Christchurch
Tel/Fax 03 366 7725

CANADA
Canadian Mental Health Association
65 Rue Brunswick Street, Suite 291,
Fredericton, New Brunswick E3B 1G5
Tel 506 455 5231 Fax 506 459 3878

The National Eating Disorder
Information Center
College Wing Room 1–211, 200
Elizabeth Street, Toronto
Ontario M5G 2C4
Tel 416 340 4156 Fax 416 340 3430

UK
British Association for Counselling
1 Regent Street, Rugby, Warwickshire
CV21 2PJ
Tel 01788 550899 / 578328 Fax 01788
562189

Cruse
Cruse House, 126 Sheen Road,
Richmond, Surrey TW9 1UP
Tel 020 8940 4818 Fax 020 8940 7638
Cruse Bereavement Line 020 8332
7227

Eating Disorders Association
Sackville Place, 44 Magdalen Street,
Norwich NR3 1JU
Tel 01603 619090 Fax 01603 664915
Helpline 01603 621414

National Childbirth Trust
Alexandra House, Oldham Terrace,
London W3 6NH
Tel 020 8992 8637

(Pax) Panic Attacks, Phobias and
Anxiety Disorders
4 Manorbrook, Blackheath, London
SE3 9AW
Tel 020 8318 5026

Relate
Herbert Gray College, Little Church
Street, Rugby, CV21 3AP
Tel 01788 573241 Fax 01788 535007

Women's Health
A Resource and Information Centre,
52 Featherstone Street,
London EC1 8RT
Tel 020 7251 6580

USA
National Eating Disorders
Organization
6655 South Yale Avenue, Tulsa,
Oklahoma 74136
Tel 918 481 4044 Fax 918 481 4076

Samaritan Befrienders
PO Box 991, Albany, WA 6330
Tel 098 422776

Index

Lynda Field books also available from Vermilion:

60 Ways to Change Your Life	£2.50
60 Ways to Feel Amazing	£2.50
The Little Book of Woman Power	£2.50
60 Tips for Self-Esteem	£6.99
Creating Self-Esteem	£6.99
60 Ways to Heal Your Life	£6.99
60 Ways to Heal Your Life	£6.99
More than 60 Ways to Make Your Life Amazing	£6.99
The Self-Esteem Workbook	£10.99

ALL VERMILION BOOKS ARE AVAILABLE THROUGH MAIL ORDER OR FROM YOUR LOCAL BOOKSHOP.

PAYMENT MAY BE MADE USING ACCESS, VISA, MASTERCARD, DINERS CLUB, SWITCH AND AMEX, OR CHEQUE, EUROCHEQUE AND POSTAL ORDER (STERLING ONLY).

EXPIRY DATE .... SWITCH ISSUE NO.

SIGNATURE ....

PLEASE ALLOW £2.50 FOR POST AND PACKING FOR THE FIRST BOOK AND £1.00 PER BOOK THEREAFTER.

ORDER TOTAL: £................................. (INCLUDING P&P)

ALL ORDERS TO:
VERMILION BOOKS, BOOKS BY POST, TBS LIMITED,
THE BOOK SERVICE, COLCHESTER ROAD, FRATING GREEN,
COLCHESTER, ESSEX, CO7 7DW, UK.

TELEPHONE: (01206) 256 000
FAX: (01206) 255 914

NAME ....

ADDRESS...

....

Please allow 28 days for delivery. Please tick box if you do not wish to receive any additional information. ☐